About This Book

Why is this topic important?

The training industry is "abuzz" with renewed conversation
tion. Some in the training industry are describing workplac
direction for the training profession to take in the future. V
esting, what trainers really do is identify skill deficiencies by
training, where appropriate, to increase a worker's skills and __ ....s has
been serving our industry well for the thirty-five years I've been in the field and I believe we
should continue in that direction.

The conversations about competencies have been going on for many more years. Every
five years or so one of many professional associations gathers a team of experts to research
training competencies. But rarely has the final step been taken to establish a certification program to encourage trainers to develop and prove their competence.

What can you achieve with this book?

This book draws on over thirty-five years of experience in training trainers by The Training
Clinic. The Training Clinic's core business is to train subject-matter experts to become trainers,
as well as course designers, facilitators, training managers, and training coordinators. It identifies real-world competencies for those who staff a training function. Trainers, facilitators,
training coaches, course designers, training coordinators, and training managers can use this
book to easily assess their skills and to create professional development plans to improve their
skill and competence and affect business results. This is the only work thus far to address competencies for training coordinators.

Organizations can use these competencies to develop their own internal training certification programs.

How is this book organized?

Each chapter begins with objectives that can be achieved by completing the chapter. To help
the reader preview a chapter, assessment questions are listed that he or she can answer by
reading the chapter. Most chapters contain extensive checklists, tools, forms, and templates
that can be printed and customized from an accompanying CD.

Competency model checklists are provided that show results or output for both basic and
advanced levels of proficiency in each competency. Following each competency model checklist, individual competencies are described, and the supporting knowledge, skills, and attitudes
needed to demonstrate each competency at both basic and advanced levels of proficiency are
listed.

The book can be read cover-to-cover, or the reader can select chapters based on a specific
interest or individual training role. The basic and advanced competencies presented in this
book describe successful behaviors of training and development professionals. The chapters are
organized around familiar training and development roles: trainer or instructor, facilitator or
coach, course designer, training manager, and training coordinator. In each chapter emerging
titles and roles for training and development professionals are also identified.

About Pfeiffer

Pfeiffer serves the professional development and hands-on resource needs of training and human resource practitioners and gives them products to do their jobs better. We deliver proven ideas and solutions from experts in HR development and HR management, and we offer effective and customizable tools to improve workplace performance. From novice to seasoned professional, Pfeiffer is the source you can trust to make yourself and your organization more successful.

Essential Knowledge Pfeiffer produces insightful, practical, and comprehensive materials on topics that matter the most to training and HR professionals. Our Essential Knowledge resources translate the expertise of seasoned professionals into practical, how-to guidance on critical workplace issues and problems. These resources are supported by case studies, worksheets, and job aids and are frequently supplemented with CD-ROMs, websites, and other means of making the content easier to read, understand, and use.

Essential Tools Pfeiffer's Essential Tools resources save time and expense by offering proven, ready-to-use materials—including exercises, activities, games, instruments, and assessments—for use during a training or team-learning event. These resources are frequently offered in loose-leaf or CD-ROM format to facilitate copying and customization of the material.

Pfeiffer also recognizes the remarkable power of new technologies in expanding the reach and effectiveness of training. While e-hype has often created whizbang solutions in search of a problem, we are dedicated to bringing convenience and enhancements to proven training solutions. All our e-tools comply with rigorous functionality standards. The most appropriate technology wrapped around essential content yields the perfect solution for today's on-the-go trainers and human resource professionals.

www.pfeiffer.com

Essential resources for training and HR professionals

For Emma Jean Barbazette and Annabelle Karen Barbazette

THE **SKILLED TRAINER** SERIES

THE TRAINER'S JOURNEY TO COMPETENCE

TOOLS, ASSESSMENTS, AND MODELS

Jean Barbazette

A Wiley Imprint
www.pfeiffer.com

For additional copies/bulk purchases of this book in the U.S. please contact 800-274-4434.
Pfeiffer books and products are available through most bookstores. To contact Pfeiffer directly call our Customer Care Department within the U.S. at 800-274-4434, outside the U.S. at 317-572-3985, fax 317-572-4002, or visit www.pfeiffer.com.
Pfeiffer also publishes its books in a variety of electronic formats. Some content that appears in print may not be available in electronic books.

ISBN: 0-7879-7523-0
Library of Congress Cataloging-in-Publication Data
Barbazette, Jean.
The trainer's journey to competence: tools, assessments, and models / by Jean Barbazette.
p. cm.—(The skilled trainer series)
Includes bibliographical references and index.
ISBN 0–7879–7523–0 (alk. paper)
1. Employees—Training of. 2. Performance standards. 3. Performance—Evaluation. I. Title. II. Series.
HF5549.5.T7B285 2005
658.3'124—dc22
2005006208

Acquiring Editor: Martin Delahoussaye
Director of Development: Kathleen Dolan Davies
Production Editor: Dawn Kilgore
Editor: Rebecca Taff
Manufacturing Supervisor: Becky Carreño

Printed in the United States of America
Printing   10   9   8   7   6   5   4   3   2   1

CONTENTS

Chapter 5: Course Designer Competencies 101

Chapter 6: Training Manager Competencies 173

Chapter 7: Training Coordinator Competencies 225

Chapter 8: Being a Department of One 269

Chapter 9: How to Develop Internal Certification Programs 277

CONTENTS OF THE CD-ROM

Competency Model Checklist for Trainers or Instructors

Expanded Competency Checklist for Trainers or Instructors

Trainer or Instructor Development Plan Template

Competency Model Checklist for Facilitators and Coaches

Expanded Competency Checklist for Facilitators and Coaches

Facilitator or Coach Development Plan Template

Competency Model Checklist for Course Designers

Expanded Competency Checklist for Course Designers

Course Designer Development Plan Template

Competency Model Checklist for Training Managers

Expanded Competency Checklist for Training Managers

Training Manager Development Plan Template

Competency Model Checklist for Training Coordinators

Expanded Competency Checklist for Training Coordinators

Training Coordinator Development Plan Template

Planning Checklist for a Department of One

Checklist for Developing a Certification Program

ACKNOWLEDGMENTS

Special thanks to Linda Ernst, Melissa Smith, Diane Fadley, Carolyn Balling, Hans Brouwer, and Kelly Barbazette for their timely suggestions and assistance. Thanks to Eileen McDargh for her creative suggestions.

Thanks to the trainers at PacifiCare Health Systems who tested several of the assessments: Lee Ann Zambrano, Norma Wienke, Teresa Cabrera, Susan Stewart, Monika Ebert, and Terri Stephens.

Thanks to my editors, Martin Delahoussaye, for believing in this project and Kathleen Dolan Davies, Rebecca Taff, and Dawn Kilgore, for their valuable suggestions.

Purpose

This book will help readers identify basic and advanced competencies for a variety of roles performed in the training function. Assessment checklists are provided that measure current basic and advanced skill levels and can be used to create a plan to develop incomplete or missing knowledge, skills, and attitudes. How to develop incomplete or missing competencies is addressed in later books that are a part of the "Skilled Trainer Series." Organizations can use the lists of competencies to create internal certificate programs for the continuing development of their training staff.

Audience

Trainers who are beyond the basics will gain the most from this book. If you are new to training, look for some useful ideas for individual development by assessing *basic* competencies. However, the trainer who has been presenting training for a year or two has experience to draw on to make a more accurate assessment of his or her current skills. If you are in this category, after assessing your *basic* competencies, move forward to assess your *advanced* competencies.

Product Description

Nine chapters provide an overview of the training function and its roles, including basic and advanced competencies for those who work in these roles. The reader is invited to assess personal skills and create an individual professional development plan. Each chapter has rich assessments, tools, and templates for personal use (these are also included on the CD-ROM accompanying the book).

A resource section and bibliography are provided at the end of the book. Suggestions for how to create an internal certification program from the competencies are also included in Chapter 8 for those who staff the training function.

Competencies Not Addressed in This Book

Additional foundational competencies for those who staff a training function are not addressed in this book because they are not *training* competencies. Some of these non-training, foundational competencies include:

- Has an understanding of the business and industry for one's organization;
- Demonstrates good verbal and written communication skills;
- Negotiates and resolves conflict assertively with others;
- Operates ethically and responsibly; and
- Keeps up-to-date with new technology.

These foundational competencies are appropriate for any person who functions in a business setting. Because they are not unique to the training and development industry, they will not be addressed here. The focus of this book is on competencies for those who staff the training function.

Product Series

This book is the first in a series of six volumes aimed at helping intermediate trainers advance their skills. Each additional book in the series will provide knowledge and skill development for one of the competencies described in this book. Enjoy the journey.

CHAPTER 1

What Is a Training Function?

Chapter Objectives

- To identify the purpose of a training function
- To describe the advantages and disadvantages of centralized and decentralized training functions
- To identify the variety of roles for those who staff a training function
  - Training managers
  - Training coordinators
  - Course designers
  - Trainers, instructors, facilitators, and coaches
- To identify the advantages and disadvantages of having full-time and part-time personnel staff the training function

Assessment Questions

- What does training accomplish?
- What are the roles in a training function?

The Purpose of a Training Function

Generally, a training function exists in an organization to develop knowledge and skills and shape attitudes that will help meet a business need. For example, often someone in the sales organization will notice that new or current salespersons lack product knowledge when new products emerge or older products are enhanced or upgraded. Often the depth of the need is assessed to determine which salespeople lack specific knowledge. Following this assessment, training may be seen as the solution to provide up-to-date information.

So a training function in a sales organization would help salespeople improve their product knowledge so that customers could select the most appropriate product to meet their needs. The training function would also help salespersons increase their sales volume by developing skills in sales techniques, time and territory management, and interpersonal skills.

Resources would be provided to develop and present a job aid, product information, or a training program. Once the salespeople became familiar with these resources, they would begin to build expertise and demonstrate success that could be measured through increased sales.

When success that results from training is not publicized or demonstrated, support for providing future resources might be withdrawn and the training function may recede into a survival mode—or even collapse. Training functions often go through this type of life cycle, illustrated in Figure 1.1.

If a training function has fulfilled the need identified at the beginning of the life cycle, then the cycle is complete and perhaps the training function ought to end. However, the real reason most training functions end or are no longer given resources is because their success and the results produced from the training function's activities are not *demonstrated* to management. Management approves funding resources, and when no new needs are assessed as justification for the training function to continue, it should rightly be closed.

The critical competencies for those who staff a training function like this one include the ability to:

- Assess training needs and develop a training plan;
- Design and present training programs that meet those needs;

Figure 1.1. Life Cycle of a Traditional Training Department

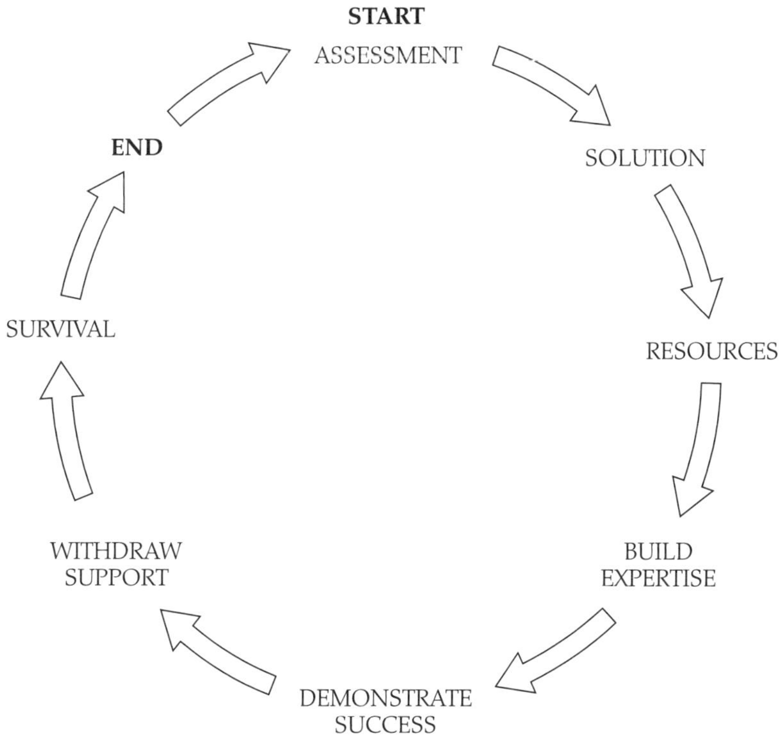

START
ASSESSMENT

SOLUTION

END

RESOURCES

SURVIVAL

WITHDRAW
SUPPORT

BUILD
EXPERTISE

DEMONSTRATE
SUCCESS

- Make sure what is learned in training is used on the job;

- Measure the results of using the improved knowledge and skills; and

- Demonstrate results to management, along with information about new or continuing training needs.

To whom the training function reports in an organization can influence what roles are required to provide appropriate training. Before further identifying roles that are needed in a training function, it would be helpful to first identify where training reports.

Centralized and Decentralized Training Functions

The two most common ways a training function reports to higher management are either as a centralized or a decentralized function. A centralized function has all trainers in an organization working in one group, with specific trainers acting as internal consultants to specific business units. The training staff reports to a training manager or chief learning officer, who often reports to a vice president of human resources. A corporate university is an example of a *centralized* training function.

A *decentralized* training function assigns or designates specific trainers acting as internal consultants to work in a business unit and report to an operating manager. The sales training example cited earlier is a decentralized function with the sales training manager reporting to the vice president of sales. In decentralized training, additional training functions would exist in the manufacturing department, corporate offices, and so forth.

Whether a training function is centralized or decentralized is not critical to the success of the function. What is critical to success is to capitalize on the advantages and work at overcoming the disadvantages. There are advantages and disadvantages to both types of organizations, summarized in Table 1.1.

Overcoming Disadvantages

Following are suggestions for the *centralized* function to overcome the disadvantages listed in Table 1.1.

1. Build relationships with the business unit you support. Make scheduled and informal visits to the department in the business unit. Identify key people who make decisions and ask them how you can support their goals.

2. Provide performance analysis assessment skills for the managers, supervisors, and lead people to distinguish between training and non-training issues. If the department personnel become adept at performance analysis, it is easier to provide the appropriate training. Learn as much as you can about the work of the business unit so subject-matter experts begin to trust your suggestions and coaching.

3. Consider the possibility of having the business unit maintain the training budget.

Table 1.1. Advantages and Disadvantages of Where a Training Function Reports

Centralized Training Function	Decentralized Training Function
Advantages	
Trainers physically located together facilitates mentoring new trainers.	Trainers find it easier to identify skill deficiencies since they "live" in the operation they support. It is easier to develop subject-matter expertise with this type of reporting.
Cross-training staff is easier to accomplish.	
It is easier to develop training specialists who have different levels of expertise.	Trainers more easily develop relationships with the business unit they support since they are present all of the time.
Experts can be developed in course development or instruction.	The supervisor who sees the results of your work in the business unit is the trainer's manager.
A career path in "training" can be developed more easily by performing in a variety of training roles.	The training budget is a line item in the department's budget and not as likely to be cut during tight financial times.
Training design and delivery are likely to be consistent.	
Disadvantages	
Trainers need to make a greater effort to develop relationships with the business unit they support since they are sometimes seen as "outsiders."	Finding another trainer as a mentor is more difficult when trainers work by themselves.
It may take longer to identify knowledge and skill deficiencies since the trainer must study the business unit from a distance and is not a subject-matter expert.	Trainers tend to be generalists who must perform a variety of roles well. This can be difficult for a new trainer whose strength is in subject-matter expertise.
The training budget for the entire organization is an easy target during cost-cutting times.	Finding a replacement or successor can be difficult if trainers are not cross-trained to function in other business units.
	Training design and delivery varies in quality and consistency.
	Some organizations have "dotted line" reporting to a central training manager, which can be confusing, be disruptive, or cause conflict.

Following are suggestions for the *decentralized* function to overcome disadvantages listed in Table 1.1.

1. Work at finding a mentor who is more skilled, expert, and capable than you, whether or not he or she is in your department. If no appropriate mentor exists in your organization, identify resources in professional associations that can help you with your development.

2. No generalist is equally adept at the variety of roles described later in this chapter. Use the checklists in later chapters to identify your strengths and weaknesses and develop a plan to grow each of these skills over time. Select the skills for development that make the greatest difference in supporting your business unit. A development template is provided at the end of each chapter.

3. Seek opportunities for cross-training and attendance at training events and conferences outside your organization.

4. If you report to a business unit manager AND have dotted line reporting to a corporate training manager, ask for clarification for which manager decides various issues. If you're not sure who makes what type of decision, look at who completes your performance and salary reviews.

Roles of the Training Function

Four main roles are needed within a training function, whether it is centralized or decentralized, so that it can develop knowledge and skills and shape attitudes that will help meet business needs. These roles include:

- Training Manager
- Training Coordinator
- Course Designer
- Trainer, Instructor, Facilitator, and Coach

Training managers are responsible for the overall working of a training function. Their responsibilities are sometimes strategic, such as planning, organizing, staffing, and budgeting, and are sometimes tactical, such as controlling training and development (T&D) operations or T&D projects and acting as internal performance consultants to link T&D operations with other organization units. For example, many training managers in large organizations present management development training for the executive groups in their organizations. Varieties of titles for a training manager include chief learning officer, learning compliance officer, or coach and mentor to newer department members.

Training coordinators are responsible for the administrative support for the training function, including ordering packaged training materials and other supplies, marketing and scheduling training, preparing classrooms for instruction, coordinating off-site facility arrangements, maintaining corporate libraries and/or resource centers, ordering and maintaining audiovisual equipment, running trainee registration/confirmation systems, monitoring tuition reimbursement programs, and summarizing course evaluation information from participants.

Course designers assess learning needs and prepare learning materials from a training plan. Materials usually include participant materials, lesson plans, audiovisual support materials, job aids, and knowledge and skill performance tests. Many course designers become *course managers,* who organize knowledge and information to make it accessible to users in a timely manner. Some course designers are designated as "owners" of a course and are responsible for evaluating the results of training and updating or revising courses as needed. The *course owner* may also be responsible for regulatory compliance reporting. Course designers often lead or act as part of a team of course developers who might create learning materials for delivery through different media. Course developers include those who write scripts and storyboards, as well as those who direct and produce computer-based or web-based programs.

Trainers or instructors present information and direct structured learning experiences so individuals increase their knowledge or skills. They prepare for instruction by reviewing course material and making minor adjustments to fit the expected target population. Trainers or instructors can also function as *facilitators* by using an indirect style that draws learning out of the students. Trainers or instructors can also function as *coaches* when assessing learner performance or when supervising learner practice sessions. Trainers can use a variety of delivery modes from one-on-one training and performance coaching to a physical classroom or distance learning in a virtual classroom.

Full-Time Versus Part-Time Personnel

The four major training roles often overlap or are combined for an individual, depending on the needs of a specific organization. The roles frequently change in scope to focus on results, not just activities. These roles can be filled by full-time staff, part-time staff, or independent contractors. Some advantages and disadvantages of having full-time versus part-time personnel staff the training function are shown in Table 1.2.

How can you determine whether your organization needs full-time or part-time staff? An easy method is to determine whether anyone functioning in one of the four part-time roles is experiencing more training requests than can be met. A needs assessment and the development of a training plan can help identify future needs. See Chapter 5 for needs assessment and training plan

Table 1.2. Advantages and Disadvantages of Full-Time and Part-Time Staff

	Advantages	Disadvantages
Full-Time Training Manager	Easier to focus on priorities within the training function	Responsibilities may not require full-time staff
Part-Time Training Manager	Cost-effective use of staff time	Conflicting operational duties take priority
Full-Time Training Coordinator	Easier to focus on priorities within the training function	Responsibilities may not require full-time staff
Part-Time Training Coordinator	Cost-effective use of staff time	Administrative details can easily be overlooked
Full-Time Course Designer	Easier to focus on priorities within the training function Designers can be assigned responsibility to update one or more courses	Responsibilities may not require full-time staff
Part-Time Course Designer	Cost-effective use of staff time	Conflicting operational duties often take priority
Full-Time Trainer	Easier to focus on priorities within the training function Trainers can become specialists in one or more courses	Responsibilities may not require full-time staff
Part-Time Trainer	Cost-effective use of staff time	Conflicting operational duties often take priority

competencies. Also, some of the suggestions in Chapter 8 about being a "department-of-one" may be useful to overcome additional disadvantages.

Overcoming Disadvantages

Here are some suggestions for those performing in each role to overcome the disadvantages listed in Table 1.2.

1. If a full-time training manager's responsibilities do not require full-time staff, the training manager can build relationships with part-time trainers and the supervisors of those trainers. An understanding about the trainers' time requirements is needed. (See additional suggestions in Chapter 6.)

2. If a part-time training manager finds that conflicting operational duties take priority, the part-time training manager can try to set aside specific office hours for training responsibilities. The part-time training manager can assign specific duties to administrative support personnel to keep training priorities on track. (See additional suggestions in Chapter 6.)

3. If a full-time training coordinator does not have full-time staff, perhaps focusing on top priorities and outsourcing training projects with lesser priority can help accomplish essential tasks. Building relationships with part-time trainers and their supervisors will also overcome the disadvantage of not having full-time staff. (See additional suggestions in Chapter 7.)

4. If a part-time training coordinator tends to overlook administrative details, using any number of software programs can effectively organize these types of details and overcome this disadvantage. Suggestions, forms, and templates are available in another book by this author, *The Trainer's Support Handbook.* (Also see additional suggestions in Chapter 7.)

5. If a full-time course designer's responsibilities do not require full-time commitment, the course designer can build relationships with training managers and trainers and identify additional development opportunities and responsibilities. Perhaps the course designer would have time to occasionally conduct some of the training and overcome this staffing disadvantage. (See additional suggestions in Chapter 5.)

6. If a part-time course designer finds that conflicting operational duties take priority, the part-time course designer can try to set aside specific office hours or blocks of time for training responsibilities to overcome this disadvantage. Assigning specific duties to administrative support personnel to keep training priorities on track can also help overcome this disadvantage. (See additional suggestions in Chapter 5.)

7. If a full-time trainer's responsibilities do not require full-time commitment, the trainer can build relationships with training managers and course designers and identify additional development opportunities and responsibilities to overcome this disadvantage. Perhaps the trainer could occasionally conduct some of the needs assessments or work on redesigning some of the out-of-date courses. (See additional suggestions in Chapter 3.)

8. If a part-time trainer finds that conflicting operational duties take priority, setting aside specific office hours or blocks of time for training responsibilities can help to overcome this disadvantage. He or she could assign specific duties to administrative support personnel to keep training priorities on track. (See additional suggestions in Chapter 3.)

CHAPTER 2

What Is a Competency?

Chapter Objectives

- To define competency
- To identify how competencies are built from knowledge and skill
- To identify what constitutes basic and advanced competence
- To measure training competencies
- To identify suggested uses for competency checklists
- To identify steps to set up a competency assessment process

Assessment Questions

- What is a competency?
- How are competencies constructed?
- How are competencies measured?

Competency Defined

Competencies are based on what a person does; they are behavioral and observable. If one is competent, then the result is effective or possibly outstanding job performance. A set of competencies is referred to as a *competency model* and is a collection of behaviors supported by underlying knowledge, skills, and attitudes that relate to a specific role or job responsibility. Building a competency model requires identifying a successful performance for a role or job responsibility and then defining the knowledge, skills, and attitudes that relate to that performance. Building a model is a collaborative process by all stakeholders.

Competency models can and do vary from one organization to another, since success is most often defined in terms of meeting a business need. Business needs differ, so competency models differ. Common themes can be found in similar roles, regardless of the industry or business need. Training and development competencies across industries and businesses also vary due to differing business needs and the organization's purpose. When considering a competency model in a specific organization, it is helpful to look at the broadest variety of behaviors, knowledge, skills, and attitudes to create your own model.

How Competencies Are Built from Knowledge and Skill

The Competency Model (Figure 2.1) is circular because a variety of knowledge, skills, and attitudes support the agreed-on behaviors and performance. Behaviors and performance can be used in any role or responsibility to create a competency model.

An example of a competency for a person with a job that includes a trainer's role is "the ability to set an adult learning climate." When selecting a competency, be sure to identify the role first. In this example, the role is a trainer. However, a course designer might also design session starters to set an adult learning climate. Next, describe the behavior; list the expected results or outputs; and identify supporting knowledge, skills, and attitudes. Provide separate descriptions for basic and advanced competencies. The following examples are a linear description of the basic climate-setting competency and a linear description of the advanced climate-setting competency.

Figure 2.1. The Competency Model

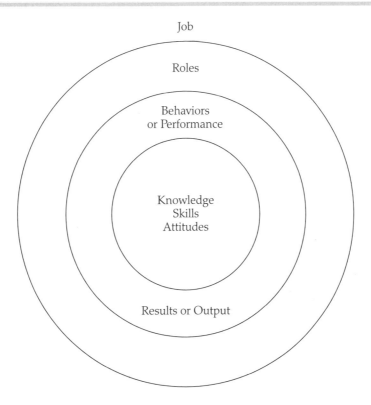

Role: Trainer

Basic Competency: Sets an Adult Learning Climate

The trainer greets participants as they enter the room and distributes handout materials and name tents. The trainer asks participants to introduce themselves and identify their objectives for the session.

Results or Output

Active participants, completed introductions, posted participant learning objectives

Supporting Knowledge

- Understands what constitutes an appropriate introduction for the trainer and the participants

Supporting Skills

- Conducts introductions that place learners at ease
- Establishes ground rules and announces the schedule for the course
- Asks for information from the learners about their objectives, experience, and motivation for the course topic

Supporting Attitudes

- Is interested in maintaining order and control
- Is interested in meeting the needs of individual participants

Role: Trainer

Advanced

Advanced Competency: Sets an Adult Learning Climate

As participants enter the physical or virtual classroom, the trainer greets them and makes a personal introduction. Copyright-free music plays, and directions to prepare for group introductions are visible. A graphic overview of the course is posted. A series of electronic slides automatically advance to reveal the theme for the course content. Participants collect or create their name tents/badges, and materials are distributed. The training session begins on time with a session starter that involves everyone in a low-risk activity that is related to the course content that follows.

Results or Output

Active participants, introductions, music, course graphic, name tents, materials, ground rules, posted objectives

Supporting Knowledge

- Is aware of role of music in setting a learning climate
- Is aware of the role of establishing ground rules at the beginning of a session
- Understands what constitutes an appropriate introduction for the trainer and the participants
- Is aware of the learners' interest in or need for making choices when entering the classroom, such as where to sit, how to complete a name tent, and so forth

- Understands what constitutes a risk for the learners
- Is aware that climate setting and resetting activities ought to be one-eighth of the course activity and that they are spaced over the length of the course

Supporting Skills

- Designs a course graphic to provide a visual overview of the course
- Selects appropriate music or other audiovisuals to play while participants assemble
- Shows electronic slides that will preview the training session concepts
- Identifies risk factors of activities relevant to the specific target population
- Conducts a session starter that involves everyone, is low risk, and is related to the course content
- Conducts introductions that place the learners at ease
- Establishes ground rules and announces the schedule for the course
- Asks for information from the learners about their objectives, experience, and motivation for learning the course topic
- Helps participants tie course objectives to a business need

Supporting Attitudes

- Is sensitive to the learners' need for inclusion in low-risk activities
- Is committed to including learners in decision making

Notice that the advanced competency description provides additional and more sophisticated methods for setting a learning climate. The outputs are greater and more effective for setting an adult learning climate. Advanced competency is built on additional knowledge, skills, and attitudes. As new knowledge and skills are acquired and new attitudes develop, it is possible for the trainer to reach a new level of competence.

How Competencies Are Measured

Being competent or not is a "pass-fail" measurement. One is either competent or one is not. Either the trainer sets an adult learning climate by being prepared, conducting introductions, and collecting learning objectives, or one of these three elements is missing and therefore the competency is not present. There is no such thing as being 70 percent competent. However, you can be competent 70 percent of the time. There is more than one way to pass or fail.

Here is an example of a rating scale to decide whether the competency is present:

A = meets *advanced* competency (advanced tangible results or output is visible)

B = meets *basic* competency (tangible results or output is visible)

I = *incomplete* (tangible results or output is not observed, missing, or partially complete)

N = behavior *not* observed (not competent)

Notice that it is possible to demonstrate different levels of a single competency. There can be different levels of performance among the competent. Both basic and advanced competencies are described in the list.

You can use competency checklists for self-assessment or to give developmental feedback to a peer or subordinate. When used in this way, it is important that the rater and the person being observed share a definition of the competencies shown on the checklist. For example, using the list of advanced competencies that follows, a trainer's idea of what constitutes "low risk" for a climate-setting activity may be different from the ideas of the person observing that trainer. Prior to rating another person using a competency checklist, review the expanded descriptions with supporting knowledge, skills, and attitudes and ensure that you share a definition of each competency.

The competency checklists in this book use verbs like "understands" or "is aware of" to describe knowledge that supports a competency. To rate a trainer's knowledge accurately, the rater and the trainer must agree prior to the rating what behaviors will demonstrate both understanding and awareness. Also, to describe attitudes that support a competency, the checklists use verbs like "is sensitive" or "is concerned." To rate the trainer's attitude accurately, the rater and the trainer must agree prior to the rating what behaviors will demonstrate these attitudes.

Decide what rating is needed to earn certification. For example, if you select twenty-two trainer competencies and seek *advanced* certification, how many competencies must be rated at the *advanced* level to earn certification? For example, The Training Clinic requires a 75 percent positive observation to earn its Certified Technical Training Specialist designation.

Suggested Uses for Competency Checklists

If your organization wishes to create an internal competency and/or certification process, begin involving management, employees, and interested groups to discuss the objectives of this type of assessment process. When rating employees represented by a collective bargaining unit, include input from the union representatives in developing the competency assessment process. Next, review all the competency checklists presented in Chapters 3 through 7 of this book. Select those competencies that are either required or desirable for the role (trainer or instructor, facilitator, coach, training manager, and training coordinator) in your organization.

Review an individual employee's job description to understand this person's role in the training function. Often competencies from more than one role are combined into a single employee's job. After selecting the appropriate competencies, copy them from the CD-ROM and create a custom competency checklist. You may want to add competencies not listed there that apply to your specific role.

Gain agreement between the rater and the person being rated about whether basic or advanced competencies are to be measured. Download the desired checklists from the CD that accompanies this book to create a customized checklist. Prior to assessing a set of competencies, identify the percent of competencies required to attest to either basic or advanced competency.

Use the assessments to develop individual development plans for each staff member. From a composite assessment, identify common developmental needs and make plans to address them. Following the development of these competencies, it may be appropriate to ask training staff to demonstrate their competency in order to take the next step toward certification. A complete discussion of internal certificate programs is in Chapter 9.

Steps to Set Up a Competency Measurement Process

Follow these steps to set up a competency measurement process using the competency checklists in this book:

1. Involve interested managers, employees, and others to agree on the objectives for a competency assessment process in your organization. Decide policy issues such as whether the process will be voluntary or mandatory, which roles will be assessed, what resources will be available for development—identified through the process and time frames. Align this process with other human resource processes such as performance appraisals and compensation and benefits programs.

2. Create a custom assessment checklist from the variety of checklists for each role in Chapters 3 through 7. Select the competencies from each role that are appropriate to a specific person's job. Add additional competencies as needed.

3. Prior to using the custom competency checklist, the rater and the person being rated should meet and agree on the common meaning of each dimension being measured.

4. Identify when and how the competencies will be observed and rated.

5. Following the observation and rating, the rater and rated person should meet to discuss the ratings. Refer to basic and advanced competency checklists for competencies rated "I" for incomplete or "N" for not observed. Discuss specific knowledge, skills, and attitudes the rater expected to see that were missing.

6. Create a development plan and agree on what resources can be committed to fulfilling the plan. Agree on when the development plan will be completed.

CHAPTER 3

Trainer or Instructor Competencies

Chapter Objectives

- To identify competencies required of a trainer or instructor
- To show how to use the competency checklists
- To create a trainer or instructor development plan

Chapter Tools

- Competency Model Checklist for Trainers or Instructors
- Expanded Competency Checklist for Trainers or Instructors
- Trainer or Instructor Development Plan Template

Assessment Questions

- What are the competencies for a trainer or instructor?
- How can these competencies be measured?
- What competencies apply to your role as a trainer or instructor?

Competencies Required of Trainers or Instructors

Trainers or instructors present information and direct structured learning experiences so individuals increase their knowledge or skills. They also facilitate learning and develop others by using coaching techniques. They prepare for instruction by reviewing course material and making minor adjustments to fit the expected target population. Trainers can use a variety of delivery modes, from one-on-one training and performance coaching to a physical classroom or distance learning in a virtual classroom. The skilled trainer is comfortable using a variety of training methods. Trainers can act as facilitators at staff meetings, at management retreats, or in other situations that require facilitation skills. (See Chapter 4 on facilitator competencies.) Trainers also have responsibilities outside the classroom, such as promoting the transfer of learning to the job and making recommendations to course designers regarding course modifications.

A variety of titles for trainers or instructors include some of these emerging titles: facilitator, knowledge specialist, learning specialist, online learning specialist, coach, learning coach, and performance improvement specialist. Coaches have special competencies, as discussed in Chapter 4.

Competency Checklists for the Trainer or Instructor

Following are two checklists that list and define broad strategic and operational competencies for the trainer or instructor. When compiled together they become a competency model for the trainer. (The titles trainer and instructor are used interchangeably for the rest of this book.)

All the competencies together describe the optimum behaviors for the trainer. When reviewing competencies for a trainer, assess whether the trainer does the tasks described. Ratings of "A" and "B" distinguish whether the competency is held at the "advanced" or "basic" level. For either an "A" or "B" rating, tangible results or outputs are visible. A rating of "I" stands for "incomplete" because tangible results or outputs are not observed, are missing, or are partially complete. Remember that competency is either observed or is not observed.

Following the Trainer or Instructor Competency Model Checklist is a second set of checklists. The first checklist expands on the numbered trainer or instructor competencies and provides a description of the *basic* competency along with supporting knowledge, skills, and attitudes. Results or output for each competency are also provided. Another checklist is provided with *advanced* competency descriptions with supporting knowledge, skills, and attitudes. At the end of the Competency Model Checklist, the rater shows the total percentage of competencies observed. Remember to decide collaboratively, prior to the observation, what percentage of competencies must be present to show competence. (See Chapter 9 for information about using competencies as part of a certification process.)

How to Use the Competency Checklists

Use competency checklists to rate yourself or as part of a collaborative process when being rated by another person. To customize the trainer competency model, first review all the checklists. Next, select those competencies that are either required or desirable for the trainer role in your organization. Download the desired checklists from the CD that accompanies this book to create a customized checklist. Either eliminate the competencies that do not apply or rate the competency as N/A for "not applicable." Prior to assessing a competency, agree with the rater on the meaning of the competencies. Review the expanded descriptions with supporting knowledge, skills, and attitudes to determine *basic* versus *advanced* levels of competency. Also, when rating another person, ensure a shared definition of each competency and what level of competency is being assessed. See the resource section at the end of this book for sample completed assessments and development plans.

Competency Model Checklist for Trainers or Instructors

A = meets *advanced* competency (advanced tangible results or outputs are visible)

B = meets *basic* competency (tangible results or outputs are visible)

I = *incomplete* (tangible results or outputs are not observed, missing or partially complete)

N = behavior *not* observed (not competent)

Rating	Trainer or Instructor Competency	Basic Results or Output	Advanced Results or Output
	1. Prepares for instruction	Training course announcement	Management partnership training course announcement
		Pre-work assignments	Pre-work assignments
		Room set-up diagram	Room set-up diagram
		Training equipment materials	Training equipment materials
	2. Sets a learning environment	Active participants, completed introductions, posted participant learning objectives.	Active participants, completed introductions, music, course graphic, name tents, materials, ground rules are set, objectives posted
	3. Uses adult learning principles	Active participants	Active participants, different training methods to appeal to different learning styles
	4. Uses lecture	Lecture notes, handout materials, visuals	Large group participation, answers participant questions, models platform techniques
	5. Conducts discussions	Agenda, questions, summary of ideas	Agenda, questions, summary of ideas, group participation
	6. Facilitates activities	Participants complete activities	Participants complete advanced activities, such as case studies, games, and simulations
	7. Conducts demonstrations	Completed product or completed process	Completed product or completed process, skill performance checklist
	8. Uses role play	Role-play observer's critique sheet, skill development	Role-play observer's critique sheet, empathy or skill development

Rating	Trainer or Instructor Competency	Basic Results or Output	Advanced Results or Output
	9. Gives feedback to learners	Negative feedback, learner changes behavior and learner improves	Positive and negative feedback, learner changes behavior and learner improves
	10. Uses audiovisuals	Equipment and media identical to handout materials	Equipment and media that support handout materials
	11. Administers tests and evaluates skill performance	Scored tests and completed skill performance checklists	Scored tests and completed skill performance checklists, timely feedback of test results
	12. Handles problem learners	Problem ignored or problem learner excluded from training	Changed learner behavior
	13. Manages appropriate use of technology	Use of technology	Use of technology
	14. Promotes learning transfer	Transferred learning is used on the job	Transferred learning is used on the job
	15. Conducts learning online	Completed lessons	Completed lessons
	16. Recommends course modifications	Written requests for changes	Written recommendations for changes
	% Total of competencies observed		
	% Total required for competence		

Expanded Competency Checklist for Trainers or Instructors

Role: Trainer or Instructor

Basic Competency 1: Prepares for Instruction

The trainer prepares to teach a specific course to a specific group by reviewing the course announcement, distributing pre-work assignments, and customizing and duplicating course materials. Closer to the training event the trainer orders equipment and sets up the training room. Online trainers would meet with a technical coordinator to confirm details of the broadcast or taping of the session.

Results or Output

Training course announcement, pre-work assignments, room set-up diagram, training equipment materials

Supporting Knowledge

- Is aware of what constitutes an appropriate pre-work assignment and how much time is needed to complete a pre-work assignment
- Is aware of optimum room set-up

Supporting Skills

- Creates and distributes appropriate pre-work assignments
- Sets up the classroom for optimum learning
- Operates classroom equipment

Supporting Attitudes

- Is willing to spend the time to complete pre-course activities
- Empathizes with participants who may not have the time to complete a pre-work assignment

Role: Trainer or Instructor

Advanced Competency 1: Prepares for Instruction

Advanced

The trainer prepares to teach a specific course to a specific group by developing a partnership with the supervisors of the participants, customizes specific examples to meet the needs of the target population. The trainer customizes the course objectives and content into benefits that appeal to the target population.

Results or Output

Management partnership, training course changes, training course announcement, pre-work assignments, room set-up diagram, training equipment materials

Supporting Knowledge

- Is aware of what constitutes an appropriate pre-work assignment and how much time is needed to complete a pre-work assignment
- Is aware of optimum room set-up
- Is aware of the role participants' managers have in the success of training
- Understands how to revise participant training materials and customize the lesson plan for this session
- Understands making benefits known to participants in a training announcement

Supporting Skills

- Partners with supervisors of participants to prepare learners for results
- Revises participant training materials based on the needs of this group
- Customizes the lesson plan to the needs of this group
- States course outcomes as benefits to the participants
- Creates and distributes appropriate pre-work assignments
- Sets up the classroom for optimum learning
- Operates classroom equipment

Supporting Attitudes

- Is willing to spend the time to complete pre-course activities
- Empathizes with participants who may not have the time to complete a pre-work assignment

Role: Trainer or Instructor

Basic Competency 2: Sets a Learning Environment

The trainer greets participants as they enter the room and distributes handout materials and name tents. The trainer asks participants to introduce themselves and identify their objectives for the session.

Results or Output

Active participants, completed introductions, posted participant learning objectives

Supporting Knowledge

- Understands what constitutes an appropriate introduction for the trainer and the participants

Supporting Skills

- Conducts introductions that place the learners at ease
- Establishes ground rules and announces the schedule for the course
- Asks for information from the learners about their objectives, experience, and motivation for the course topic

Supporting Attitudes

- Is interested in maintaining order and control

Role: Trainer or Instructor

Advanced Competency 2: Sets a Learning Environment

As participants enter the physical or virtual classroom, the trainer or instructor greets them and makes a personal introduction. Copyright-free music plays, and directions to prepare for group introductions are visible. A graphic overview of the course is posted as a course map. A series of electronic slides automatically advance to reveal the theme for the course content. Participants collect or create their name tents/badges, and materials are distributed. The training session begins with a session starter that involves everyone in a low-risk activity that is related to the course content that follows.

Results or Output

Active participants, completed introductions, music, course graphic, name tents, materials, ground rules are set, objectives posted

Supporting Knowledge

- Is aware of role of music in setting a learning climate
- Is aware of the role of established ground rules at the beginning of a session
- Understands what constitutes an appropriate introduction for the trainer and the participants
- Is aware of the learners' interest in making choices when entering the classroom, such as where to sit, how to complete a name tent, and so on
- Understands what constitutes a risk for the learners
- Is aware that climate-setting activities ought to be one eighth of the course activity

Supporting Skills

- Designs a course graphic to provide a visual overview of the course
- Selects appropriate music or other audiovisuals to play while participants assemble
- Shows electronic slides that will preview the training session concepts

- Identifies risk factors of activities relevant to the specific target population
- Conducts a session starter that involves everyone, is low risk, and is related to the course content
- Conducts introductions that place the learners at ease
- Establishes ground rules and announces the schedule for the course
- Asks for information from the learners about their objectives, experience, and motivation for the course topic
- Helps participants tie course objectives to a business need

Supporting Attitudes

- Is sensitive to the learners' need for inclusion in low-risk activities
- Includes the learners in decision making

Role: Trainer or Instructor

Basic Competency 3: Uses Adult Learning Principles

The trainer or instructor uses adult learning principles that enhance motivation and improve retention.

Results or Output

Active participants

Supporting Knowledge

- Is aware of the importance of building learning on an adult's experiences

Supporting Skills

- Provides a practical and useful learning experience

Supporting Attitudes

- Respects participants' prior knowledge and skills

Role: Trainer or Instructor

Advanced

Advanced Competency 3: Uses Adult Learning Principles

The trainer or instructor uses adult learning principles that enhance motivation and improve retention, that use a variety of learning methods, and that set a collaborative learning environment.

Results or Output

Active participants, different training methods to appeal to different learning styles

Supporting Knowledge

- Is aware of the importance of building learning on an adult's experiences
- Understands learning styles and the importance of using a variety of training methods
- Is aware of the importance of helping participants identify the benefits of learning something new
- Understands which adult learning principles are a priority for a specific target population

Supporting Skills

- Provides a practical and useful learning experience
- Acknowledges participants' prior knowledge and skills
- Uses a variety of training methods

Supporting Attitudes

- Respects participants' prior knowledge and skills
- Is willing to give up some control of the learning situation to build a collaborative learning experience

Role: Trainer or Instructor

Basic Competency 4: Uses Lecture

The trainer or instructor gives a lecture that is well organized, easy to follow, contains enough clear and accurate examples, and contains a visual component through handout materials and visuals.

Results or Output

Lecture notes, handout materials, visuals

Supporting Knowledge

- Understands appropriate visual support for verbal information
- Understands appropriate examples
- Is aware of logical structure

Supporting Skills

- Sets up the lecture by telling the objective and gives an overview of the content
- Provides clear and accurate examples
- Supplements verbal comments with written handout materials and visuals

Supporting Attitudes

- Is interested in being logical and well-organized

Role: Trainer or Instructor

Advanced

Advanced Competency 4: Uses Lecture

The trainer involves learners approximately every fifteen minutes, handles questions well, and uses appropriate platform techniques.

Results or Output

Large group participation, answers participant questions, models platform techniques

Supporting Knowledge

- Understands appropriate visual support for verbal information
- Understands appropriate examples
- Is aware of logical structure
- Is aware of an adult's attention span
- Understands how to ask questions that promote reflection and learning

Supporting Skills

- Sets up the lecture by telling the objective and gives an overview of the content
- Provides clear and accurate examples
- Supplements verbal comments with written handout materials and visuals
- Answers questions accurately
- Involves learners in brief activities at least every fifteen minutes
- Maintains eye contact and uses appropriate gestures
- Avoids distracting words, such as "ah," "um," and "ya' know"
- Varies speaking rate, pitch, and volume
- Has learners develop or use the concepts from the lecture
- Has learners finish the lecture or make a summary or application of the ideas presented

Supporting Attitudes

- Is interested in being logical and well-organized
- Appreciates that all lectures will not be liked by all adults
- Is willing to keep lectures short and to a minimum during a course

Role: Trainer or Instructor

Basic Competency 5: *Conducts Discussions*

The trainer or instructor controls the discussion by asking appropriate questions, includes all participants by asking direct questions and answers questions from participants. The trainer provides a complete summary of the main points

Results or Output

Agenda, questions, summary of ideas

Supporting Knowledge

• Understands the interactions during a dynamic discussion

Supporting Skills

• Sets up the discussion by stating the objective and gives an overview of the agenda

• Asks overview questions to begin the discussion

• Asks direct questions to gain fuller participation

• Asks participants to clarify the concepts

• Makes a summary

Supporting Attitudes

• Is willing to remain impartial so participants will expresses their own opinions

Role: Trainer or Instructor

Advanced Competency 5: Conducts Discussions

The trainer conducts a discussion by asking appropriate questions to clarify and expand the topic, including all participants, keeping the group on track, and calling for a consensus or summary. The trainer uses redirected and reverse questions to involve all participants

Results or Output

Agenda, questions, summary of ideas, group participation

Supporting Knowledge

- Understands interactions during a dynamic discussion
- Is aware of what constitutes a facilitative role for a discussion leader
- Understanding the interactions during a dynamic discussion
- Understands how to ask questions that promote reflection and learning

Supporting Skills

- Sets up the discussion by stating the objective and gives an overview of the agenda
- Asks overhead questions to begin the discussion
- Asks direct, redirected, and reverse questions to gain fuller participation
- Asks a variety of open and closed questions to appropriately direct the discussion
- Challenges generalizations and irrelevant digressions and probes for deeper meaning
- Draws out quiet or reluctant participants without embarrassing the learner
- Asks participants to clarify the concepts and make a summary

Supporting Attitudes

- Is willing to remain impartial so participants will express their own opinions
- Is patient

Role: Trainer or Instructor

Basic Competency 6: Facilitates Exercises

The trainer or instructor sets up the activity by giving clear directions, groups participants, and draws learning points from the participants. The trainer makes a summary of key points.

Results or Output

Participants complete activities

Supporting Knowledge

- Understands the importance of learning by doing

Supporting Skills

- Sets up the learning activity by telling the objective and gives an overview of the activity
- Groups participants and assigns roles appropriate to the activity
- Observes the participants and assists groups as needed
- Conducts a debriefing to stress learning points
- Makes a summary of key points

Supporting Attitudes

- Is willing to use a variety of activities to reach all learners

Role: Trainer or Instructor

Advanced

Advanced Competency 6: Facilitates Exercises, Case Studies, Games, and Simulations

The trainer sets up the activity by giving clear directions, groups participants, and draws learners' reactions and learning points from the participants. The trainer helps the participants apply what is learned from these activities.

Results or Output

Participants complete advanced activities, such as case studies, games, and simulations

Supporting Knowledge

- Understands the importance of learning by doing
- Understands how to group learners for the best results
- Understands which types of questions will help learners discover concepts and apply new learning
- Understands how to refocus groups that become lost or distracted during an activity
- Is aware that unexpected learning can occur

Supporting Skills

- Sets up the learning activity by telling the objective and gives an overview of the activity without revealing what the learners will discover
- Groups participants and assigns roles appropriate to the activity
- Observes the participants and assists groups as needed
- Conducts a debriefing of the activity by asking participants to share and interpret their reactions to the activity by asking appropriate questions
- Asks participants to identify learning points that usually emerge from the activity
- Handles unexpected learning appropriately
- Asks participants to identify how they will use or apply the concepts learned from the activity

Supporting Attitudes

- Is willing to use a facilitative role and not be too directive or controlling

Role: Trainer or Instructor

Basic Competency 7: *Conducts Demonstrations*

The trainer conducts a demonstration to show the correct way to complete a process or a procedure while explaining what the participants hear and see. The trainer supervises participants in a return demonstration, asking questions, giving feedback, and making corrections. The trainer summarizes key points.

Results or Output

Completed product or completed process

Supporting Knowledge

- Understands the process or procedure to be demonstrated

Supporting Skills

- Sets up the demonstration by telling the objective and gives an overview of the process or procedure to be demonstrated

- Shows the process or procedure while explaining what learners see and hear

- Supervises participant return demonstrations, gives feedback, and makes corrections

- Supervises practice sessions to complete learning

- Evaluates learning through tests

Supporting Attitudes

- Shows concern for the participants' safety

Role: Trainer or Instructor

Advanced Competency 7: Conducts Demonstrations

The trainer conducts a demonstration to show the correct way to complete a process or a procedure while explaining what the participants hear and see. The trainer supervises participants in a return demonstration, asking questions, giving feedback, and making corrections. The trainer asks questions to have the learners summarize key points.

Results or Output

Completed product or completed process, skill performance checklist

Supporting Knowledge

- Understands the process or procedure to be demonstrated
- Is aware of the risk to participants of doing or learning the process or procedure
- Understands how much practice is required to learn a new skill based on task difficulty, the importance of doing the task in a standardized manner, and the frequency with which the task is done on the job
- Is aware of participant sensitivity to feedback
- Understands how to ask questions that promote reflection and learning

Supporting Skills

- Sets up the demonstration by telling the objective and gives an overview of the process or procedure to be demonstrated
- Shows the process or procedure while explaining what learners see and hear
- Supervises participant return demonstrations, gives feedback, and makes corrections
- Supervises practice sessions to complete learning
- Evaluates learning through appropriate skill performance tests

- Asks appropriate questions
- Asks learners questions so learners develop concepts and make a summary

Supporting Attitudes

- Shows concern for the participants' safety
- Is sensitive to participants who receive feedback

Role: Trainer or Instructor

Basic Competency 8: Uses Role Play

The trainer sets up and structures the role play to promote skill practice. The trainer might role play the skill with a participant in front of the group as a model of the skill being taught.

Results or Output

Role play observer's critique sheet, skill development

Supporting Knowledge

- Is aware of what constitutes an appropriate role model

Supporting Skills

- Sets up the role play by sharing the objective, selecting a volunteer, and preparing the volunteer for his or her role

- Makes a summary of skills demonstrated

Supporting Attitudes

- Shows concern to present an authentic role model

Role: Trainer or Instructor

Advanced **Advanced Competency 8: Uses Role Play**

The trainer sets up and structures the role play in groups of three to promote empathy or skill practice. The instructor and peers observe participants and give feedback to promote learning and application of skills on the job.

Results or Output

Role-play observer's critique sheet; empathy or skill development

Supporting Knowledge

- Is aware of the risk factors of participant skill practice during a role play
- Understands how to minimize risk and promote the benefits of role play
- Understands how to ask questions that promote reflection and learning

Supporting Skills

- Sets up the role play by sharing the objective, selecting characters, and preparing the characters for their roles
- Structures the role play to be completed simultaneously in groups of three.
- Instructs observers and provides a checklist for completion during the observation
- Asks participants to play the scene without over-directing
- Asks participants to share and interpret their reactions to the role plays
- Asks participants questions to develop the concept of empathy or focus on the skills being developed
- Asks participants questions to summarize and apply what was learned to the job

Supporting Attitudes

- Shows empathy
- Makes the environment safe, not embarrassing for the learner

Role: Trainer or Instructor

Basic Competency 9: Gives Feedback to Learners

The trainer corrects the learners' mistakes by telling the correct way to complete an activity, process, or procedure.

Results or Output

Negative feedback to learner, learner changes behavior, and learner improves

Supporting Knowledge

• Understands how feedback affects a learner's performance

Supporting Skills

• Describes specifically what the learner does and says that is incorrect
• Offers an appropriate model

Supporting Attitudes

• Is helpful

Role: Trainer or Instructor

Advanced ***Advanced Competency 9: Gives Feedback to Learners***

As part of the learning process, trainers give feedback to learners. Positive feedback reinforces what is done well and negative feedback is given to correct what is not done correctly. Feedback is given without making the learner defensive.

Results or Output

Positive and negative feedback; learner changes behavior and learner improves

Supporting Knowledge

- Is aware of how to give feedback so the learner does not become defensive
- Is aware of whether the learner is capable of the desired performance

Supporting Skills

- Describes specifically what the learner does and says, rather than focusing on attitude or placing a value on it or making a judgment
- Focuses on limited issues and avoids describing behavior as "always" or "never"
- Focuses on behavior the learner can do something about
- Gives well-timed information
- Uses paraphrasing to ensure learner understanding and clear communication
- Helps learners gain insights and verbalize the rationale for changed behavior

Supporting Attitudes

- Is willing to focus on behavior, not attitude
- Is willing to be helpful, not intrusive

Role: Trainer or Instructor

Basic Competency 10: Uses Audiovisuals

The trainer selects audiovisual media that support the learning objective. Visuals are often identical to training handout materials. The trainer receives help from technicians who troubleshoot mechanical problems.

Results or Output

Equipment and media identical to handout materials

Supporting Knowledge

- Is aware of what type of media support a learning objective
- Is aware of who and how to call for technical support or troubleshooting

Supporting Skills

- Shows or customizes visual images that support the learning objective

Supporting Attitudes

- Is willing to make the most effective use of media

Role: Trainer or Instructor

Advanced **Advanced Competency 10: Uses Audiovisuals**

Visuals show appropriate and accurate images and copy. When showing visuals, the trainer supports the content, rather than replacing it. The trainer operates equipment with ease and troubleshoots minor mechanical problems effectively. The trainer respects the copyright ownership of others' materials.

Results or Output

Equipment and media that support handout materials

Supporting Knowledge

- Is aware of what type of media support a learning objective
- Is aware of who and how to call for technical support or troubleshooting
- Is aware of different learning styles that need visual support for conceptual information
- Understands the importance of color to create emphasis and retain information
- Familiar with how to operate frequently used equipment

Supporting Skills

- Shows or customizes visual images that support the learning objective
- Selects a variety of media to enhance different learning styles
- Uses color appropriately
- Does not read to the learner from the visuals
- Operates equipment with ease, and troubleshoots minor mechanical problems

Supporting Attitudes

- Is willing to make the most effective use of media

Role: Trainer or Instructor

Basic Competency 11: Administers Tests and Evaluates Skill Performance

The trainer limits test content to material already taught in the course by distributing written test materials efficiently and at the right time. The trainer gives clear directions, monitors participant progress, and answers questions.

Results or Output

Scored tests and completed skill performance checklists

Supporting Knowledge

- Is aware of what content is appropriate for testing
- Understands the testing process

Supporting Skills

- Selects appropriate content and test items
- Administers the test fairly

Supporting Attitudes

- Is willing to be fair

Role: Trainer or Instructor

Advanced

Advanced Competency 11: Administers Tests and Evaluates Skill Performance

The trainer limits test content to material already taught in the course by distributing written test materials efficiently and at the right time. The trainer gives clear directions, monitors participant progress, and answers questions without providing unwarranted assistance. The trainer collects and corrects the tests in a timely manner to provide feedback to the learners.

Results or Output

Scored tests and completed skill performance checklists, timely feedback of test results

Supporting Knowledge

- Is aware of what content is appropriate for testing
- Understands the testing process
- Is aware of methods participants could use to cheat during a test
- Understands how to give feedback regarding incorrectly answered test items
- Is aware of how to make a skill performance observation as objective as possible

Supporting Skills

- Selects appropriate content and test items
- Administers the test fairly
- Answers participant questions without providing unwarranted assistance
- Corrects tests promptly
- Provides feedback to learners to improve performance
- Makes skill performance observations using an objective checklist

Supporting Attitudes

- Is willing to be fair
- Recognizes some participants may attempt to cheat on a test
- Is willing to be helpful appropriately

Role: Trainer or Instructor

Basic Competency 12: Handles Problem Learners

The trainer uses two strategies to deal effectively with learners who act inappropriately or disrupt the learning process.

Results or Output

Problem ignored or problem learner excluded from training

Supporting Knowledge

- Is aware of the source of problem learner behavior

Supporting Skills

- Uses high-risk disciplinary strategies to correct problem learner behavior
- Ignores minor problem learner behaviors and talks to disruptive participants privately
- Uses interactive training methods to redirect the focus of a problem learner
- Asks disruptive participants to leave the classroom

Supporting Attitudes

- Is willing to ignore minor disruptive behavior
- Unwilling to accept verbal or physical abuse from learners

Role: Trainer or Instructor

Advanced

Advanced Competency 12: Handles Problem Learners

The trainer uses four or more strategies to deal effectively with learners who act inappropriately and disrupt the learning process.

Results or Output

Changed learner behavior

Supporting Knowledge

- Is aware of the source of problem learner behavior

- Understands the risk associated with various problem learner strategies

Supporting Skills

- Identifies whether or not a problem is caused by the content or process of instruction

- Anticipates problem learners by using prevention strategies, such as setting ground rules

- Ignores minor problem learner behaviors and takes corrective action when appropriate

- Uses interactive training methods to redirect the focus of problem learners

- Uses high-risk disciplinary strategies to correct problem learner behavior as a last resort

- Assesses the effectiveness of problem learner strategies

Supporting Attitudes

- Is willing to confront disruptive behavior assertively

- Is unwilling to allow anyone to disrupt the learning of others

- Is unwilling to accept verbal or physical abuse from learners

Role: Trainer or Instructor

Basic Competency 13: Manages Appropriate Use of Technology

Trainer makes the best use of available technology to present courses.

Results or Output

Use of technology

Supporting Knowledge

- Understands the capabilities of technology owned by the organization

Supporting Skills

- Operates software and hardware that are a part of the course
- Provides written directions for others to operate technical tools
- Seeks support for technical assistance

Supporting Attitudes

- Is willing to ask for help from technical support

Role: Trainer or Instructor

Advanced **Advanced Competency 13: Manages Appropriate Use of Technology**
Trainer uses the most up-to-date available technology to present courses.
Trainer uses a combination of blended learning delivery modes when
appropriate.

Results or Output

Use of technology

Supporting Knowledge

- Is aware of research that supports the use of technology as an effective
  learning tool

- Understands the capabilities of different types of technology

Supporting Skills

- Smoothly operates software and hardware that are a part of the course

- Places learners at ease when introducing new technology through
  learning activities

- Provides written and verbal directions for others to operate technical
  tools

- Interacts appropriately with technical support personnel

- Completes system and sound checks prior to conducting a course

Supporting Attitudes

- Is willing to practice using technology before using it in the classroom

- Shows patience with less proficient learners

- Is willing to ask for help from technical support

Role: Trainer or Instructor

Basic Competency 14: Promotes Learning Transfer

The trainer uses a variety of strategies and tactics to promote learning transfer to the job during the course.

Results or Output

Transferred learning is used on the job

Supporting Knowledge

- Is aware of the trainer's role in transferring new learning to the job
- Understands assessment tools
- Is aware of a variety of techniques to partner with learners during training to promote learning transfer

Supporting Skills

- Uses adult learning methods to facilitate content that addresses the participants' real issues
- Provides appropriate practice and feedback to learners

Supporting Attitudes

- Is willing to work with learners during training to make a connection between training and the use of skills on the job

Role: Trainer or Instructor

Advanced *Advanced* **Competency 14: *Promotes Learning Transfer***

The trainer uses a variety of strategies and tactics to promote learning transfer to the job before, during, and after the course.

Results or Output

Transferred learning is used on the job

Supporting Knowledge

- Is aware of the trainer's role, participants' role, and the role of the participants' manager in transferring new learning to the job

- Understands assessment tools

- Is aware of a variety of techniques to partner with learners and their managers to promote learning transfer

Supporting Skills

- Sets objectives with the participants' manager that are based on needs defined with the manager

- Customizes content to meet the participants' needs

- Uses adult learning methods to facilitate content that addresses the participants' real issues

- Provides appropriate practice and feedback to learners

- Provides follow-up information to assist coaching and support by the participants' managers

- Assists the managers in evaluating the transfer of learning and bottom-line results of training

Supporting Attitudes

- Is willing to extend the trainer's role in transferring learning beyond the classroom

---

Role: Trainer or Instructor

 Basic Competency 15: Conducts Learning Online

The trainer conducts courses in a virtual classroom using synchronous and asynchronous tools.

Results or Output

Completed lessons

Supporting Knowledge

- Is aware of how to use a few tools of the technology appropriate for synchronous or asynchronous courses
- Limited understanding of how the technology works
- Is aware of the differences in how to use a few training methods in a virtual classroom

Supporting Skills

- Uses lecture appropriately in a virtual classroom
- Helps learners become familiar with a few tools in the technology by pointing them out
- Facilitates threaded discussions
- Uses appropriate visual support

Supporting Attitudes

- Is willing to be thoroughly prepared
- Is helpful to new learners

Role: Trainer or Instructor

Advanced *Advanced Competency 15: Conducts Learning Online*

The trainer conducts courses in a virtual classroom using a variety of synchronous and asynchronous tools.

Results or Output

Completed lessons

Supporting Knowledge

- Is aware of which tools of the technology are appropriate for synchronous or asynchronous courses

- Understands how the technology works

- Is aware of the differences in how to use classroom training methods in a virtual classroom

Supporting Skills

- Uses a variety of training methods appropriately in a virtual classroom

- Helps learners become familiar with tools in the technology that promote participation by using them

- Compensates for a lack of face-to-face contact appropriately

- Departs from the prepared script to promote learning

- Facilitates threaded discussions

- Uses appropriate visual support

Supporting Attitudes

- Is willing to be thoroughly prepared

- Helpfulness to new learners

Role: Trainer or Instructor

Basic Competency 16: Recommends Course Modifications

The trainer assesses the effectiveness of a course and requests that the course designer make appropriate changes.

Results or Output

Written requests for changes

Supporting Knowledge

- Is aware of the variety of factors that influence the effectiveness of training
- Understands when to request a change to a course

Supporting Skills

- Identifies appropriate changes to make a course more effective
- Identifies when a course does not match the job and is out-of-date

Supporting Attitudes

- Is interested in having the course up-to-date

Role: Trainer or Instructor

Advanced **Advanced Competency 16: Recommends Course Modifications**

The trainer assesses the effectiveness of a course and makes specific recommendations for course changes to the course designer and training manager.

Results or Output

Written recommendations for changes

Supporting Knowledge

- Is aware of the variety of factors that influence the effectiveness of training
- Understands when to make a recommendation to change a course
- Is aware of how to state recommendations to avoid a defensive reaction
- Understands course design principles

Supporting Skills

- Identifies appropriate changes to make a course more effective
- Identifies when a course does not match the job and is out-of-date
- Tactfully makes appropriate recommendations for course changes

Supporting Attitudes

- Interest in making a course more effective

Trainer or Instructor Development Plan

Following the completion of a competency checklist, create a development plan that identifies the trainer's strengths, identifies areas for coaching and feedback, and identifies missing knowledge and skills, along with resources for development. Beginning a development plan with a trainer's strengths acknowledges this person's strengths that can be built on. Strengths can also be used to mentor others. Areas for coaching and feedback can be competencies that were not observed. They may be competencies that require more practice because the trainer may already have supporting knowledge and attitudes, but did not display the skill. Areas that are missing can be deficient because some knowledge, skills, or attitudes are missing. Refer to the secondary checklists to identify what is missing and to plan what resources are available to build these competencies.

Gain agreement from management for the commitment of resources for development. Agree on a time frame for the development and re-evaluation of the competency.

A sample Trainer or Instructor Development Plan Template is on the next page.

Trainer or Instructor Development Plan Template

Trainer's Name: _____   Date:_____

1. List competencies that exceed expectation:

2. Identify

Underdeveloped or unobserved competencies	Knowledge, skills, and attitudes to acquire

3. Identify competencies that require coaching and feedback:

4. Identify resources required to develop these competencies:

Target date for re-evaluation:

_____

CHAPTER 4

Facilitator or Coach Competencies

Chapter Objectives

- To identify competencies required of a facilitator or coach
- To learn how to use the competency checklists
- To create a facilitator or coach development plan

Chapter Tools

- Competency Model Checklist for Facilitators and Coaches
- Expanded Competency Checklist for Facilitators and Coaches
- Facilitator or Coach Development Plan Template

Assessment Questions

- What are the competencies for a facilitator or coach?
- How can these competencies be measured?
- What competencies apply to your role as a facilitator or coach?

Competencies Required of Facilitators or Coaches

Like trainers or instructors, facilitators and coaches direct structured learning experiences so that individuals increase their knowledge or skills. They also facilitate learning in a less directive manner and develop others by using coaching techniques.

Facilitators and coaches can use a variety of delivery modes from one-on-one meetings and performance coaching to delivery in a physical classroom or meeting room or meetings facilitated in a virtual room. The skilled facilitator or coach is comfortable using a variety of methods. Facilitators can preside at staff meetings, management retreats, or other situations that require facilitation skills.

A variety of titles for facilitators and coaches include some of these emerging titles: facilitator, process facilitator, content facilitator, meeting facilitator, retreat leader, coach, learning coach, and performance improvement specialist.

Competency Checklists for the Facilitator or Coach

Following are two checklists that list and define broad strategic and operations competencies for the facilitator or coach. When compiled together they become a competency model for the facilitator or coach.

All the competencies together describe the optimum behaviors for a facilitator or coach. When reviewing competencies for a facilitator or coach, assess whether the facilitator or coach does the tasks described. Ratings of "A" and "B" distinguish whether the competency is held at the "advanced" or "basic" level. For either an "A" or "B" rating, tangible results or outputs are visible. A rating of "I" stands for "incomplete" because tangible results or outputs are not observed, are missing, or are partially complete. Remember that competency is either observed or is not observed.

Following the Facilitator or Coach Competency Model Checklist is a second set of checklists. The first checklist expands on the numbered facilitator or coach competencies and provides a description of the *basic competency*, along with supporting knowledge, skills, and attitudes. Results or output for each competency are also provided. Another checklist is provided with *advanced competency* descriptions with supporting knowledge, skills, and attitudes. At the end of the Competency Model Checklist the rater shows the total percentage of competencies observed. Remember to decide prior to the observation what percentage of competencies must be present to show competence. See Chapter 9 for information about using competencies as part of a certification process.

How to Use the Competency Checklists

To customize the facilitator or coach competency model, first review all the checklists. Next, select those competencies that are either required or desirable for the facilitator or coach role in your organization. Download the desired checklists from the CD that accompanies this book to create a customized checklist. Either eliminate the competencies that do not apply or rate the competency as N/A for "not applicable." Prior to assessing a competency, agree with the rater on the meaning of the competencies. If unsure whether to measure a basic or an advanced competency, download both descriptions. If the checklists are not for a self-assessment, review the expanded descriptions with supporting knowledge, skills, and attitudes to ensure a shared definition of each competency and what level of competency is being assessed. See the resource section at the end of this book for sample completed assessments and development plans.

Competency Model Checklist for Facilitators and Coaches

A = meets *advanced* competency (advanced tangible results or outputs are visible)

B = meets *basic* competency (tangible results or outputs are visible)

I = *incomplete* (tangible results or outputs are not observed, missing or partially complete)

N = behavior *not* observed (not competent)

Rating	Facilitator Competencies	Basic Results or Output	Advanced Results or Output
	1. Plans team or training meetings using an agenda	Facilitator's agenda	Collaborative agenda
	2. Sets a productive climate and begins a discussion	Participants are ready to begin a discussion	Participants are ready to begin a discussion, collaboratively set ground rules
	3. Gets the group to focus on defining and reaching outcomes	Defined outcomes Plan to reach outcomes	Defined outcomes Variety of processes to reach outcomes
	4. Helps group communicate effectively	Effective group communication Group harmony	Effective group communication Open and civil disagreement
	5. Encourages creative problem solving, including brainstorming	List of brainstormed options Solved problems	List of brainstormed options Variety of problem-solving techniques Solved problems
	6. Supports and encourages participation	Partial group participation	Complete, non-defensive group participation
	7. Fosters self-discovery of alternatives and solutions	Participants find alternatives and solutions	Participants find alternatives and solutions Inventories
	8. Helps the group make decisions	Group makes a decision Facilitator's rationale	Group reaches a decision, by consensus when appropriate Group's rationale
	9. Selects a team leader	Team leader selected by the facilitator	Team leader selected by the group
	10. Handles disruptive participants effectively excluded from the group	Problem ignored or problem member	Behavior change

Rating	Coaching Competencies	Basic Results or Output	Advanced Results or Output
	1. Builds a relationship	Participants accept coaching	Participants willingly accept coaching
	2. Provides information	Shared expertise	Shared information
	3. Facilitates development	Participants develop skills	Participants develop skills through self-discovery
	4. Confronts when necessary	Participants overcome inaction Facilitator removes learning obstacles	Participants overcome inaction Suggests how the learner can remove obstacles
	5. Deals with change	Change occurs	Change effected successfully
	% Total of competencies observed		
	% Total required for competence		

Expanded Competency Checklists for Facilitators and Coaches

Role: Facilitator

Basic Competency 1: *Plans Team or Training Meetings Using an Agenda*

The facilitator plans a team or training meeting using an agenda that contains objectives and content items for discussion and resolution by the group.

Results or Output

Facilitator's agenda

Supporting Knowledge

- Understands how to set an agenda
- Is aware of what can be accomplished during a given meeting
- Understands additional planning steps needed for a specific meeting

Supporting Skills

- Circulates the agenda prior to the meeting

Supporting Attitudes

- Is efficient

Role: Facilitator

Advanced

Advanced Competency 1: Plans Team or Training Meetings Using an Agenda

The facilitator plans a team or training meeting using an agenda that contains objectives and content items for discussion and resolution by the group. The agenda is a collaborative product and distributed to all participants prior to the meeting.

Results or Output

Collaborative agenda

Supporting Knowledge

- Understands collaborative agenda-setting techniques
- Is aware of what can be accomplished during a given meeting
- Understands additional planning steps needed for a specific meeting

Supporting Skills

- Solicits agenda items from participants
- Ties agenda items to a business need
- Contacts participants from prior meetings to obtain updated information and completed assignments
- Circulates the agenda prior to the meeting

Supporting Attitudes

- Is willing to share decision making
- Is thorough and persistent

Role: Facilitator

 ### Basic Competency 2: Sets a Productive Climate and Begins a Discussion

The facilitator uses a few techniques to set a productive climate for the group and begins a discussion appropriately.

Results or Output

Participants are ready to begin a discussion

Supporting Knowledge

- Is aware of the needs and interests of group members
- Understands how to use questions to begin a discussion

Supporting Skills

- Sets a productive climate through room set-up
- Sets ground rules
- Begins a meeting with an appropriate introduction of a new topic or an update on a continuing matter

Supporting Attitudes

- Is interested in placing participants at ease
- Is willing to enforce ground rules

Role: Facilitator

Advanced Competency 2: Sets a Productive Climate and Begins a Discussion

The facilitator uses a variety of techniques to set a productive climate for the group and begins a discussion appropriately.

Results or Output

Participants are ready to begin a discussion, collaboratively set ground rules

Supporting Knowledge

- Is aware of the needs and interests of group members
- Understands climate-setting activities that would lead this group toward beginning a discussion
- Understands how to use questions to begin a discussion
- Understands awkwardness of the group during the "forming" stage[1]

Supporting Skills

- Sets a productive climate through room set-up
- Collaboratively sets ground rules
- Places new group members at ease through an appropriate introduction that acknowledges expertise
- Begins a meeting with an appropriate introduction of a new topic or an update on a continuing matter
- Asks appropriate questions to initiate the discussion

Supporting Attitudes

- Is interested in placing participants at ease
- Fosters cooperation
- Is willing to enforce ground rules
- Is willing to share decision making

---

[1]Bruce W. Tuckman, "Development Sequences in Small Groups," *Psychological Bulletin*, 1965.

Role: Facilitator

Basic Competency 3: Gets the Group to Focus on Defining and Reaching Outcomes

The facilitator gets the group to define outcomes or objectives for the project or a specific meeting. The facilitator recommends a plan to reach the outcomes to the group.

Results or Output

Defined outcomes, plan to reach outcomes

Supporting Knowledge

- Is aware of a few techniques to help groups be productive
- Understands the basics of group dynamics

Supporting Skills

- Charts suggestions and ideas from the group
- Asks questions to bring clarity or develop a topic
- Organizes and presents information from the group to form a plan
- Makes a summary for the group

Supporting Attitudes

- Is willing to get the group to be productive

Role: Facilitator

Advanced ### Advanced Competency 3: Gets the Group to Focus on Defining and Reaching Outcomes

The facilitator uses a variety of activities to define outcomes or objectives for the project or a specific meeting. The facilitator encourages team members to create a plan to reach the outcomes.

Results or Output

Defined outcomes, plan to reach outcomes, variety of processes to reach outcomes

Supporting Knowledge

- Is aware of a variety of techniques to help groups to be productive
- Understands group dynamics at the storming, norming, and performing stages of team development[2]
- Understands factors that foster appropriate decision making

Supporting Skills

- Charts suggestions and ideas from the group
- Asks questions to bring clarity or develop a topic
- Uses brainstorming and other idea-development techniques to keep the group thinking divergently
- Organizes information from the group into a plan
- Helps the group to summarize and reach a decision by consensus where appropriate
- Uses time efficiently to help groups summarize
- Keeps the group on track and bars irrelevant diversions
- Helps the group through storming and norming phases of group development to reach the performing and productive stages

Supporting Attitudes

- Is willing to let the group arrive at a plan of their creation
- Is willing to facilitate, rather than direct

---

[2]Bruce W. Tuckman, "Development Sequences in Small Groups," *Psychological Bulletin*, 1965.

Role: Facilitator

Basic Competency 4: Helps Group Communicate Effectively

The facilitator encourages all group members to participate and understand one another's points of view.

Results or Output

Effective group communication

Supporting Knowledge

- Understands paraphrase, active listening, and question techniques

Supporting Skills

- Initiates, proposes, and makes suggestions that bring clarity to the communication
- Accurately records group member ideas
- Organizes information

Supporting Attitudes

- Is willing to let others speak and clarify meaning

Role: Facilitator

Advanced Competency 4: Helps Group Communicate Effectively

The facilitator encourages all group members to participate and understand one another's points of view.

Results or Output

Effective group communication, group harmony, open and civil disagreement

Supporting Knowledge

- Is aware of group dynamics
- Understands paraphrase, active listening, and question techniques

Supporting Skills

- Initiates, proposes, and makes suggestions that bring clarity to the communication
- Uses paraphrase and questions to clarify meaning
- Accurately records group member ideas
- Encourages divergent thinking and uses a variety of idea-generation techniques
- Organizes information
- Encourages diverse opinions and facts from reluctant participants
- Keeps the conversation civil, even with disagreement
- Acknowledges all points of view

Supporting Attitudes

- Encourages original and diverse thinking
- Is willing to let others speak and clarify meaning
- Is willing to challenge irrelevant or hostile comments

Role: Facilitator

Basic Competency 5: Encourages Creative Problem Solving, Including Brainstorming

The facilitator helps the group to engage in creative problem solving through brainstorming.

Results or Output

List of brainstormed options, solved problems

Supporting Knowledge

- Understands brainstorming rules
- Is aware of when to use specific creative-problem-solving techniques

Supporting Skills

- Conducts brainstorming sessions
- Helps participants identify problems
- Directs participants in reaching a decision

Supporting Attitudes

- Is willing to enforce brainstorming rules

Role: Facilitator

Advanced **Advanced Competency 5: Encourages Creative Problem Solving, Including Brainstorming**

The facilitator helps the group to engage in creative-problem-solving techniques, including brainstorming.

Results or Output

List of brainstormed options, variety of problem-solving techniques, solved problems

Supporting Knowledge

- Understands brainstorming rules
- Understands creative and linear problem solving
- Is aware of when to use specific creative-problem-solving techniques
- Recognizes that every issue is not a problem

Supporting Skills

- Conducts brainstorming sessions
- Helps participants identify problems
- Uses a variety of creative techniques to help participants to identify solutions
- Keeps the problem solving divergent until enough ideas are generated
- Assists participants in reaching a decision

Supporting Attitudes

- Is willing to allow a creative process the time to generate ideas
- Is willing to enforce brainstorming rules

Role: Facilitator

Basic Competency 6: Supports and Encourages Participation

The facilitator uses a few techniques to support and encourage participation by all group members.

Results or Output

Partial group participation

Supporting Knowledge

- Understands questioning and listening techniques

Supporting Skills

- Asks appropriate questions
- Initiates, proposes, and makes suggestions
- Charts group ideas
- Draws out quiet participants using direct questions

Supporting Attitudes

- Encourages participation

Role: Facilitator

Advanced

Advanced Competency 6: Supports and Encourages Participation

The facilitator uses a variety of techniques to support and encourage participation by all group members. Reluctant participants are drawn out using non-defensive techniques

Results or Output

Complete, non-defensive group participation

Supporting Knowledge

- Understands group dynamics
- Understands questioning and listening techniques
- Understands the risk factors for group members to participate

Supporting Skills

- Asks appropriate questions
- Initiates, proposes, and makes suggestions
- Divides participants into subgroups to increase participation
- Encourages diverse opinions and facts from reluctant participants
- Organizes a sequence of speakers
- Charts group ideas
- Draws out quiet participants in a non-defensive manner

Supporting Attitudes

- Is sensitive to the preferences of some group members to listen, rather than participate through discussion
- Is willing to use low-risk activities that encourage participation

Role: Facilitator

Basic Competency 7: Fosters Self-Discovery of Alternatives and Solutions

The facilitator uses questions to help participants to create alternatives, suggestions, and solutions.

Results or Output

Participants find alternatives and solutions

Supporting Knowledge

- Is aware of different questioning techniques

Supporting Skills

- Uses questions appropriately
- Uses brainstorming
- Encourages participants to reach a conclusion

Supporting Attitudes

- Controls the group process

Role: Facilitator

Advanced

Advanced Competency 7: Fosters Self-Discovery of Alternatives and Solutions

The facilitator uses questions and other techniques to help participants to create alternatives, suggestions, and solutions.

Results or Output

Participants find alternatives and solutions, inventories

Supporting Knowledge

- Is aware of a variety of techniques that lead participants to discover alternatives

- Understands group dynamics

Supporting Skills

- Uses questioning appropriately

- Uses brainstorming and other creative-problem-solving methods

- Assigns specific tasks to subgroups to foster self-discovery

- Uses inventories and questionnaires as a means of fostering self-discovery of alternatives

- Uses convergent techniques to help participants to decide on a solution

Supporting Attitudes

- Encourages the group's knowledge, skills, and talents to lead the group, rather than controlling the process

- Is willing to handle unexpected learning

Role: Facilitator

Basic Competency 8: Helps the Group Make Decisions

The facilitator helps the group reach a decision and summarizes the group's rationale.

Results or Output

Group reaches a decision

Supporting Knowledge

- Understands how to help others evaluate points of view
- Understands why and how to influence others to change their minds
- Understands voting techniques and how to surface majority and minority opinions

Supporting Skills

- Helps the group summarize areas of agreement
- Uses questions to clarify majority and minority viewpoints

Supporting Attitudes

- Is interested in reaching a decision

Role: Facilitator

Advanced **Advanced Competency 8: Helps the Group Make Decisions**

The facilitator helps the group reach a decision and gets the group to provide rationales for its decisions. The facilitator uses decision by consensus when appropriate.

Results or Output

Group reaches a decision based on its rationale, including by consensus when appropriate

Supporting Knowledge

- Recognizes that consensus decision making is not appropriate for all decisions the group will make
- Understands how to help others evaluate points of view
- Understands why and how to influence others to change their minds
- Is aware of when to recommend a different type of decision-making technique
- Understands group dynamics and how to help a group to be productive

Supporting Skills

- Helps the group summarize areas of agreement
- Uses questions to clarify points of difference
- Uses a variety of techniques to be sure all points of view are explained
- Asks questions to help build a consensus when appropriate
- Asks the group to provide a rationale for its decision

Supporting Attitudes

- Is willing to invest the time required for consensus building
- Is willing to be indirect when appropriate

Role: Facilitator

Basic Competency 9: Selects a Team Leader

The facilitator selects a team leader agreeable to the group.

Results or Output

Team leader selected by the facilitator

Supporting Knowledge

- Understands how to recruit volunteers
- Understands team leadership selection criteria

Supporting Skills

- Gains agreement for the leadership choice

Supporting Attitudes

- Is interested in strong leadership

Role: Facilitator

Advanced

Advanced Competency 9: Selects a Team Leader

The facilitator helps the group to select an appropriate and skilled team leader.

Results or Output

Team leader

Supporting Knowledge

- Understands group dynamics and the stages of team development
- Understands team leadership selection criteria

Supporting Skills

- Solicits group input for leadership criteria
- Asks questions to help the group evaluate team leader candidates
- Collaboratively helps group to choose a team leader

Supporting Attitudes

- Is willing to allow the group to choose its own leader

Role: Facilitator

Basic Competency 10: Handles Disruptive Participants Effectively

The facilitator uses two strategies to deal with group members who act inappropriately and disrupt the meeting.

Results or Output

Problem ignored or member excluded from the group

Supporting Knowledge

- Is aware of the source of problem participant behavior

Supporting Skills

- Uses high-risk disciplinary strategies to correct problem participant behavior
- Asks disruptive participants to leave the classroom

Supporting Attitudes

- Is willing to ignore minor disruptive behavior
- Is unwilling to accept verbal or physical abuse from others

Role: Facilitator

Advanced

Advanced Competency 10: Handles Disruptive Participants Effectively

The facilitator uses four or more strategies to deal effectively with group members who act inappropriately and disrupt the meeting.

Results or Output

Behavioral change

Supporting Knowledge

- Is aware of what causes disruptive behavior
- Understands the risk associated with various problem participant strategies

Supporting Skills

- Identifies whether or not a problem is caused by the content or process of the meeting
- Anticipates disruptive group members by using prevention strategies, such as setting ground rules
- Ignores minor problem behaviors and takes corrective action when appropriate
- Uses interactive methods to redirect the focus of a disruptive participant
- Uses high-risk disciplinary strategies to correct disruptive behavior as a last resort
- Assesses the effectiveness of strategies

Supporting Attitudes

- Is willing to confront disruptive behavior assertively
- Is unwilling to allow anyone to disrupt the learning of others
- Is unwilling to accept verbal or physical abuse from learners

Role: Coach

Basic Competency 1: Builds a Relationship

The coach establishes and builds a relationship with the learner or employee so that suggestions and guidance are acted on.

Results or Output

Participant accepts coaching

Supporting Knowledge

- Understands how to build a relationship

Supporting Skills

- Establishes a relationship

- Listens to the learner

- Asks questions

Supporting Attitudes

- Is patient

- Is willing to establish an ongoing relationship

Role: Coach

Advanced Competency 1: Builds a Relationship

Advanced

The coach establishes and builds a relationship with the learner or employee so that suggestions and guidance are acted on.

Results or Output

Participants willingly accepts coaching

Supporting Knowledge

- Understands the difference between coaching and directing
- Understands how to build a relationship
- Is aware of factors that build trust

Supporting Skills

- Establishes a relationship
- Builds trust
- Listens to the learner
- Asks questions
- States support in a positive manner
- Makes and keeps commitments

Supporting Attitudes

- Is patient
- Is willing to establish an ongoing relationship

Role: Coach

Basic Competency 2: *Provides Information*

The coach shares information, guidance, and direction to influence the learner. The coach often shares stories from experience and recommends specific approaches.

Results or Output

Shared expertise

Supporting Knowledge

- Understands what type of expertise is appropriate to share

Supporting Skills

- Provides information that is useful and well-timed
- Shares information that is specific to an issue
- Provides timely suggestions
- Gives directions
- Gives guidance

Supporting Attitudes

- Is helpful

Role: Coach

Advanced Competency 2: Provides Information

The coach shares information to influence the learner. If the learner has skill, often identifying an issue or providing some information can assist the learner in moving forward without being over-directed.

Results or Output

Shared information

Supporting Knowledge

- Understands how to offer information
- Is aware that some learners do not like being over-directed

Supporting Skills

- Provides information that is useful and well-timed
- Shares information that is specific to an issue
- Helps learner brainstorm information and approaches
- Breaks down expertise and complex information so it is usable to a new performer
- Provides timely suggestions
- Avoids guiding and directing by asking appropriate questions
- Allows learner to partner in learning by seeking information

Supporting Attitudes

- Is willing to limit information to a specific issue
- Is helpful

Role: Coach

Basic Competency 3: Facilitates Development

The coach makes observations, offers suggestions, provides resources, and encourages the learner to develop specific skills.

Results or Output

Participant develops skills

Supporting Knowledge

- Is aware of adult learning model
- Understands when to offer suggestions or provide information rather than demonstrate or train

Supporting Skills

- Offers suggestions and advice that are appropriate and timely
- Makes personal introductions to resources
- Provides answers and anticipates questions

Supporting Attitudes

- Is helpful
- Encourages others

Role: Coach

Advanced **Advanced Competency 3: Facilitates Development**

The coach makes observations, offers suggestions, provides resources, and encourages the learner to develop specific skills. The coach partners with the learner through questions and self-discovery techniques.

Results or Output

Participant develops skills through self-discovery

Supporting Knowledge

- Is aware of adult learning model
- Understands when to offer suggestions or provide information rather than demonstrate or train
- Understands how to partner with the learner to promote self-discovery

Supporting Skills

- Offers suggestions that are appropriate and timely without intruding
- Provides appropriate and accessible resources for self-discovery and independent learning
- Asks questions rather than provides answers
- Encourages learner to develop a plan and set deadlines

Supporting Attitudes

- Is helpful
- Encourages others
- Is interested in self-discovery by the learner

Role: Coach

Basic Competency 4: Confronts When Necessary

The coach recognizes when the learner is procrastinating or delaying necessary steps to complete a process or move forward in a project. The coach confronts the learner with questions and makes recommendations and suggestions.

Results or Output

Participant overcomes inaction; facilitator removes obstacles to learning

Supporting Knowledge

- Is aware of when confrontation would be helpful
- Understands the obstacles that inhibit movement or development

Supporting Skills

- Asks questions
- Provides general suggestions and recommendations
- Removes obstacles for the learner

Supporting Attitudes

- Is willing to confront a learner to facilitate effect development
- Is willing to remove obstacles to learning

Role: Coach

Advanced Competency 4: Confronts When Necessary

The coach recognizes when the learner is procrastinating or delaying necessary steps to complete a process or move forward in a project. The coach confronts the learner with factual observations, asks questions, and makes recommendations and suggestions. He or she encourages the learner to remove or overcome obstacles.

Results or Output

Participant overcomes inaction; coach suggests how the learner can remove obstacles

Supporting Knowledge

- Is aware of when confrontation would be helpful
- Understands the obstacles that inhibit movement or development

Supporting Skills

- Makes observations
- Asks questions
- Provides specific and narrow suggestions and recommendations
- Encourages learners to identify and remove obstacles for themselves
- Links rewards to progress and positive behavior

Supporting Attitudes

- Is willing to confront a learner to bring about development
- Is willing to let the learner struggle to remove obstacles
- Is patient

Role: Coach

Basic Competency 5: Deals with Change

The coach provides encouragement to the learner to take necessary risks, offers suggestions and recommendations to more forward. The coach identifies how to help the learner attain comfort with the changes he or she is facing.

Results or Output

Change occurs

Supporting Knowledge

- Is aware of some of the stages of change a learner goes through when faced with a situation that requires a change

Supporting Skills

- Offers suggestions to deal with the discomfort that accompanies change
- Identifies benefits of making changes happen

Supporting Attitude

- Shows empathy

Role: Coach

Advanced Competency 5: Deals with Change

The coach provides encouragement to the learner to take necessary risks, offers suggestions and recommendations to more forward. The coach identifies how to help the learner attain comfort with doing something differently once changes have occurred.

Results or Output

Change effected successfully

Supporting Knowledge

- Understands the stages of change a learner goes through when faced with a situation that requires a change

- Understands the difference between successful change (the change occurs) and effective change (the change occurs willingly)

- Understands the impact on self-esteem from change

- Understands how to help a learner move forward and become more comfortable with changes

Supporting Skills

- Helps learners analyze a situation that requires change

- Offers suggestions to deal with the discomfort that accompanies change

- Helps learners identify benefits of making changes happen

- Encourages the learner to practice doing something differently to reinforce changed behavior

Supporting Attitudes

- Is willing to make changes in oneself

- Shows empathy

Facilitator or Coach Development Plan

Following the completion of a competency checklist, create a development plan that identifies the facilitator's or coach's strengths, identifies areas for coaching and feedback, and identifies missing knowledge and skills, along with resources for development. Beginning a development plan with a facilitator's or coach's strengths acknowledges this person's strengths that can be built on for further development. Strengths can also be used to mentor others. Areas for coaching and feedback can be competencies that were not observed. They may be competencies that require more practice because the facilitator or coach may already have supporting knowledge and attitudes, but did not display the skill. Areas that are missing can be deficient because some knowledge, skills, or attitudes are missing. Refer to the secondary checklists to identify what is missing and to plan what resources are available to build these competencies.

Gain agreement from management for the commitment of resources for development. Agree on a time frame for the development and re-evaluation of the competency.

A sample Facilitator or Coach Development Plan Template is on the next page.

Facilitator or Coach Development Plan Template

Facilitator's or Coach's Name: _____ Date: _____

1. List competencies that exceed expectation:

2. Identify

Underdeveloped or unobserved competencies	Knowledge, skills, and attitudes to acquire

3. Identify competencies that require coaching and feedback:

4. Identify resources required to develop these competencies:

Target date for re-evaluation:

CHAPTER 5

Course Designer Competencies

Chapter Objectives

- To identify competencies required of a course designer
- To learn how to use the competency checklists
- To create a course designer development plan

Chapter Tools

- Competency Model Checklist for Course Designers
- Expanded Competency Checklist for Course Designers
- Course Designer Development Plan Template

Assessment Questions

- What are the competencies for training course designers?
- How can these competencies be measured?
- What competencies apply to your role as a course designer?

Competencies Required of Course Designers

Course designers are responsible for assessing training needs and designing training programs to meet the organization's needs. Competencies required for an effective course designer are planning, developing, and evaluating training courses.

Planning competencies include assessing training needs and developing a training plan that includes learning objectives. *Developing* competencies include creating course content, selecting appropriate learning methods, making sequencing and pacing considerations, developing materials, and creating a lesson plan. *Evaluating* competencies typically means that the trainer learns how to use Donald Kirkpatrick's four-level model.

A variety of titles used for course designers include some of these emerging titles: chief knowledge officer, instructional systems designer, online learning developer, and performance technologist.

Competency Checklists for Course Designers

Following are two checklists that list and define the planning, developing, and evaluating competencies for course designers. Together they become a competency model for the course designer.

All the competencies together describe the optimum behaviors for the course designer. When reviewing competencies for a course designer, assess whether the course designer does the tasks described. Ratings of "A" and "B" distinguish whether the competency is held at the "advanced" or "basic" level. For either an "A" or "B" rating, tangible results or outputs are visible. A rating of "I" stands for "incomplete" because tangible results or outputs are not observed, are missing, or are partially complete. Remember that competency is either observed or is not observed.

Following the Course Designer Competency Model Checklist is the second set of checklists. The first of these expands on the numbered course designer competencies and provides a description of the *basic* competency along with supporting knowledge, skills, and attitudes. Results or output for each competency are also provided. Another checklist is provided with *advanced* competency descriptions with supporting knowledge, skills, and attitudes. At the end of the Competency Model Checklist, the rater shows the total percentage of competencies observed. Remember to decide prior to the observation what percentage of competencies must be present to show competence. See Chapter 9 for information about using competencies as part of a certification process.

How to Use the Competency Checklists

Use competency checklists to rate yourself or as part of a collaborative process when being rated by another person. To customize the course designer competency model, first review all the checklists. Next, select those competencies that are either required or desirable for the course designer role in your organization. Download the desired checklists from the CD that accompanies this book to create a customized checklist. Either eliminate the competencies that do not apply or rate the competency as N/A for "not applicable." Prior to assessing a competency, agree with the rater on the meaning of the competencies. Review the expanded descriptions with supporting knowledge, skills, and attitudes to determine *basic* versus *advanced* levels of competency. Also, when rating another person, ensure a shared definition of each competency and what level of competency is being assessed. See the resource section at the end of this book for sample completed assessments and development plans.

Competency Model Checklist for Course Designers

A = meets *advanced* competency (advanced tangible results or outputs are visible)

B = meets *basic* competency (tangible results or outputs are visible)

I = *incomplete* (tangible results or outputs are not observed, missing or partially complete)

N = behavior *not* observed (not competent)

Rating	Course Designer Competency	Basic Results or Output	Advanced Results or Output
	Planning Competencies: Needs Assessment		
	1. Uses performance analysis to sort training and non-training issues	Training recommendations	Performance analysis report
	2. Uses target population analysis to identify critical elements about the intended participants	Target population statement Recommendations	Target population statement Recommendations
	3. Conducts a "needs versus wants" analysis to identify common needs of a specific target population	Data summary Recommendations	Data summary Recommendations
	4. Conducts a job analysis to identify critical job success elements	Data summary Recommendations	Data summary Recommendations
	5. Conducts a task analysis to break a task into its teachable parts	Task breakdown	Task breakdown
	6. Creates a skill hierarchy to identify supporting skills and course prerequisites	Skill hierarchy Course prerequisites	Skill hierarchy Course prerequisites
	7. Writes terminal and enabling learning objectives that meet four criteria	Terminal and enabling course objectives	Terminal and enabling course objectives
	8. Facilitates a feedback meeting to interpret data	Recommendations	Shared recommendations
	Planning Competencies: Training Plan		
	9. Identifies the training issue and how it relates to a business need	Training plan to justify a training event request	Training plan issues related to a business need

Rating	Course Designer Competency	Basic Results or Output	Advanced Results or Output
	10. States the outcome, results, and objectives of the training	Training event rationale	Training plan results
	11. States the performance deficiency and its causes	Training event justification	Performance deficiencies and causes
	12. Identifies or establishes performance standards	Performance standards	Performance standards
	13. Identifies the target population	Target population statement	Target population statement
	14. Establishes criteria to evaluate the training	Evaluation tools	Evaluation tools
	15. Describes the proposed intervention	Training event description	Variety of activities and interventions Job aids
	16. Estimates the cost of the training plan	Estimated costs	Feasibility cost estimate
	17. Builds a partnership with management to ensure success of the training plan	Training announcement	Partnership roles
	18. Schedules training	Training schedule	Training schedule
	**Developing Training Competencies**		
	19. Creates a broad content outline	Content outline	Content outline
	20. Identifies sources for course content	Resources	Resources
	21. Selects appropriate methods	Methods	Methods based on knowledge, skill, or attitudinal objectives
	22. Sequences training methods	Sequenced training methods	Sequenced training methods
	23. Ensures a variety of pacing for training methods	Variety of training methods	Pacing plan

Rating	Course Designer Competency	Basic Results or Output	Advanced Results or Output
	24. Identifies how much practice is required to learn a new skill	Practice exercises	Practice plan
	25. Writes training activities	Written activities	Written activities
	26. Identifies the appropriate type of lesson plan for a specific course	Template for lesson plan	Template for lesson plan
	27. Writes the lesson plan	Lesson plan	Lesson plan
	28. Conducts a pilot workshop and makes appropriate revisions	Pilot workshop Course revisions	Pilot workshop Course revisions
	Evaluation Competencies		
	29. Designs a reaction sheet to get feedback from participants	Reaction sheet	Reaction sheet
	30. Writes a test to measure learning	Test	Valid and reliable test
	31. Creates a skill performance checklist to measure the transfer of learning to the workplace	Skill performance checklist	Skill performance checklist
	32. Creates a return on investment analysis to identify results	Collected cost information	Analysis

% Total of competencies observed

% Total required for competence

Expanded Competency Checklist for Course Designers

Role: Course Designer

Basic Needs Assessment Competency 1: Uses Performance Analysis to Sort Training and Non-Training Issues

Asks questions to identify which issues are training needs and which are non-training needs. Recommends training solutions where appropriate.

Results or Output

Training recommendations

Supporting Knowledge

- Understands what type of questions are appropriate
- Is aware of appropriate people to interview

Supporting Skills

- Asks appropriate questions
- Distinguishes between training and non-training issues
- Makes recommendations for training issues

Supporting Attitudes

- Is willing to have developed data determine the outcome and recommendations

Role: Course Designer

Advanced **Advanced Needs Assessment Competency 1: Uses Performance Analysis to Sort Training and Non-Training Issues**

Conducts a performance analysis to identify which issues are training needs and which are non-training needs. Recommends training solutions where appropriate.

Results or Output

Performance analysis report

Supporting Knowledge

- Understands informal and formal methodologies to conduct a performance analysis
- Understands what type of questions are appropriate
- Is aware of appropriate people to interview
- Understands survey techniques to collect and interpret statistically significant data

Supporting Skills

- Uses informal and formal performance analysis tools appropriately
- Asks appropriate questions
- Distinguishes between training and non-training issues
- Makes recommendations for training issues
- Addresses non-training issues
- Ties training recommendations to business needs

Supporting Attitudes

- Is willing to have developed data determine the outcome and recommendations
- Is interested in conserving resources for true training needs
- Is interested in the deeper or root causes of issues or problems

---

Role: Course Designer

Basic Needs Assessment Competency 2: Uses Target Population Analysis to Identify Critical Elements About the Intended Participants

Identifies information to make appropriate content and grouping decisions.

Results or Output

Target population statement, recommendations

Supporting Knowledge

- Is aware of which people or employees constitute the target population
- Is aware of information to seek about the target population
- Understands the decisions that will be made based on the data collected

Supporting Skills

- Asks appropriate questions
- Interviews a sufficient number of the target population to make appropriate recommendations
- Writes justifications for content selection and grouping decisions based on the data

Supporting Attitude

- Shows sensitivity to the needs of the target population

Role: Course Designer

Advanced Needs Assessment Competency 2: Uses Target Population Analysis to Identify Critical Elements About the Intended Participants

Identifies information in six critical areas to make appropriate content and grouping decisions.

Results or Output

Target population statement, recommendations

Supporting Knowledge

- Is aware of which people or employees constitute the target population
- Is aware of different types of information to seek about the target population
- Understands the decisions that will be made based on the data collected
- Understands what constitutes appropriate questions for a specific target population
- Understands survey techniques to collect and interpret statistically significant data

Supporting Skills

- Asks appropriate questions
- Interviews a sufficient number of the target population to make appropriate recommendations
- Collects information through surveys when appropriate
- Writes justifications for content selection and grouping decisions based on the data and the business needs

Supporting Attitudes

- Is sensitive to the needs of the target population
- Avoids making the target population defensive and unwilling to answer questions

Role: Course Designer

 Basic Needs Assessment Competency 3: Conducts a "Needs Versus Wants" Analysis to Identify Common Needs of a Specific Target Population

Creates a list of desired skills the target population may need or want and surveys the population to identify common needs.

Results or Output

Data summary, recommendations

Supporting Knowledge

- Is aware of whom to survey
- Is aware of which types of content topics to list in a survey

Supporting Skills

- Creates a survey of training topics
- Collects and summarizes survey data
- Makes recommendations on which courses would be appropriate from the data

Supporting Attitudes

- Is open-minded
- Shows flexibility in making interpretations from the data

Role: Course Designer

Advanced

Advanced Needs Assessment Competency 3: Conducts a "Needs Versus Wants" Analysis to Identify Common Needs of a Specific Target Population

Identifies a list of desired skills the target population may need or want and surveys the population to identify common needs. Identifies which managers and subordinates of the target population might be surveyed to gain additional perspectives of the target population's training needs.

Results or Output

Data summary, recommendations

Supporting Knowledge

- Is aware of whom to survey
- Is aware of which types of content topics to list in a survey
- Is aware of survey techniques to create valid recommendations
- Understands survey techniques to collect and interpret statistically significant data

Supporting Skills

- Creates an appropriate survey that can be taken online or in hard copy
- Collects and synthesizes data
- Conducts a feedback meeting with the client sponsors and/or managers to help interpret data
- Makes recommendations on which courses would be appropriate from the data and based on business needs

Supporting Attitudes

- Is open-minded
- Is flexible in making interpretations from the data
- Is interested in the deeper or root causes of issues or problems

---

Role: Course Designer

 Basic Needs Assessment Competency 4: Conducts a Job Analysis to Identify Critical Job Success Elements

With assistance from subject-matter experts, analyzes job elements to identify critical tasks required to perform a job successfully.

Results or Output

Data summary, recommendations

Supporting Knowledge

- Is aware of job elements
- Is aware of what makes a task critical
- Understands interviewing and questioning skills

Supporting Skills

- Uses keen observation skills to record a task
- Asks questions of subject-matter experts to identify critical tasks in a job
- Summarizes data
- Makes course content recommendations

Supporting Attitude

- Is interested in creating a thorough and accurate report or job profile

Role: Course Designer

Advanced Competency 4: Conducts a Job Analysis to Identify Critical Job Success Elements

Analyzes job elements to identify critical tasks required to perform a job successfully.

Results or Output

Data summary, recommendations

Supporting Knowledge

- Is aware of job elements
- Understands what makes a task critical
- Understands hierarchies
- Understands interviewing and questioning skills

Supporting Skills

- Asks basic and follow-up questions of subject-matter experts to identify critical tasks in a job
- Summarizes data
- Makes course content recommendations based on data and business needs

Supporting Attitude

- Is interested in creating a thorough and accurate report or job profile

Role: Course Designer

Basic ***Basic Needs Assessment Competency 5: Conducts a Task Analysis to Break a Task into Its Teachable Parts***

With the help of subject-matter experts, analyzes task elements to identify critical steps required to perform a task successfully.

Results or Output

Task breakdown

Supporting Knowledge

- Is aware of job elements
- Is aware of what makes a task critical
- Understands interviewing and questioning skills
- Understands how to complete a task observation and documentation

Supporting Skills

- Lists the critical steps in performing a specific task
- Asks a subject-matter expert to estimate the difficulty of doing the task by a typical performer
- Observes and interviews a master performer while he or she does the task
- Validates documentation by making a final observation

Supporting Attitude

- Is interested in being accurate and complete in documentation

Role: Course Designer

Advanced Needs Assessment Competency 5: Conducts a Task Analysis to Break a Task into Its Teachable Parts

Analyzes task elements to identify critical steps required to perform a task successfully.

Results or Output

Task breakdown

Supporting Knowledge

- Is aware of job elements
- Understands what makes a task critical
- Understands hierarchies
- Understands interviewing and questioning skills
- Understands how to complete a task observation and documentation

Supporting Skills

- Lists the critical steps in performing a specific task
- Estimates the difficulty of doing the task by a typical performer
- Observes and interviews a master performer while he or she does the task
- Asks basic and follow-up questions of master performers to gain an understanding of critical tasks
- Validates documentation by making a final observation

Supporting Attitudes

- Is interested in being accurate and complete in documentation

Role: Course Designer

Basic Needs Assessment Competency 6: Creates a Skill Hierarchy to Identify Supporting Skills and Course Prerequisites

With assistance from subject-matter experts, arranges task steps in a sequential order. Places supporting skills under each step to show the relationship of a skill to a task step. Identifies course prerequisites and areas for learning objectives.

Results or Output

Skill hierarchy, course prerequisites

Supporting Knowledge

- Is aware of how to construct and read a skill hierarchy
- Is aware of factors to consider in recommending course prerequisites and areas for developing learning objectives

Supporting Skills

- Arranges skills in an appropriate hierarchy for each step in a task
- Validates the hierarchy with the help of a subject-matter expert
- Identifies course prerequisites
- Identifies areas for developing learning objectives

Supporting Attitude

- Is willing to balance interests of the target population and the client in determining course prerequisites

Role: Course Designer

Advanced **Advanced Needs Assessment Competency 6: Creates a Skill Hierarchy to Identify Supporting Skills and Course Prerequisites**

Arranges task steps in a sequential order. Places supporting skills under each step to show the relationship of a skill to a task step. Identifies course prerequisites and areas for learning objectives.

Results or Output

Skill hierarchy, course prerequisites

Supporting Knowledge

- Is aware of how to construct and read a skill hierarchy
- Is aware of factors to consider in recommending course prerequisites and areas for developing learning objectives

Supporting Skills

- Arranges skills in an appropriate hierarchy for each step in a task
- Validates the hierarchy independently or as needed, with the help of a subject-matter expert
- Identifies course prerequisites
- Identifies areas for developing learning objectives

Supporting Attitude

- Is willing to balance interests of the target population and the client in determining course prerequisites

Role: Course Designer

Basic Needs Assessment Competency 7: Writes Terminal and Enabling Learning Objectives That Meet Four Criteria

Based on a task analysis and skills hierarchy, writes terminal and enabling objectives.

Results or Output

Terminal and enabling course objectives

Supporting Knowledge

- Is aware of at least two of the four criteria for writing learning objectives (written from the learner's point of view, specific behavior, condition, and level of achievement)

- Is aware of the relationship between terminal and enabling objectives

Supporting Skills

- Interprets task analysis and skill hierarchy data correctly

- With assistance, writes terminal and enabling learning objectives that meet four criteria

- Validates completeness of terminal and enabling learning objectives with a senior course designer

Supporting Attitude

- Is determined and focused to write specific, behavioral learning objectives.

Role: Course Designer

 Advanced ***Advanced Needs Assessment Competency 7: Writes Terminal and Enabling Learning Objectives That Meet Four Criteria***

Based on a task analysis and skills hierarchy, writes terminal and enabling objectives that meet four criteria.

Results or Output

Terminal and enabling course objectives

Supporting Knowledge

- Understands the four criteria for writing learning objectives (written from the learner's point of view, specific observable behavior, condition, and level of achievement)

- Is aware of the relationship between terminal and enabling objectives

- Is aware of the difference between learning objectives and job performance objectives

- Understands how learning objectives are related to job objectives and business needs

Supporting Skills

- Interprets task analysis and skill hierarchy data correctly

- Writes terminal and enabling learning objectives that meet four criteria

Supporting Attitudes

- Is determined and focused to write learning objectives, rather than job objectives

Role: Course Designer

Basic Needs Assessment Competency 8: Facilitates a Feedback Meeting to Interpret Data

Interprets survey data and makes recommendations for training projects to management.

Results or Output

Recommendations

Supporting Knowledge

- Is aware of pre-survey opinions of training program sponsors and supervisors

Supporting Skills

- Analyzes data
- Asks appropriate questions
- Makes recommendations based on survey data

Supporting Attitude

- Is willing to justify data interpretation

Role: Course Designer

Advanced Needs Assessment Competency 8: Facilitates a Feedback Meeting to Interpret Data

Conducts a feedback meeting with training program sponsors and supervisors (and perhaps target population representatives) to interpret survey data and gain agreement on project objectives.

Results or Output

Shared recommendations

Supporting Knowledge

- Is aware of how to conduct a feedback meeting
- Is aware of pre-survey opinions of training program sponsors and supervisors
- Understands survey techniques to collect and interpret statistically significant data

Supporting Skills

- Analyzes data
- Asks appropriate questions
- Encourages others to rationalize data interpretations
- Helps a group to reach consensus and support group recommendations
- Makes recommendations based on survey data and business needs

Supporting Attitudes

- Is willing to discuss alternative interpretations of data
- Is determined to encourage consensus decision making rather than forcing choices on group members

Role: Course Designer

Basic Planning Competency 9: Identifies the Training Issue and How It Relates to a Business Need

Training needs are explored, training issues extracted and documented. A training plan is written that provides solutions to the problems brought to the training organization.

Results or Output

Training plan

Supporting Knowledge

- Is aware of the difference between issues, problems, and needs
- Is aware of the difference between symptoms and problems

Supporting Skills

- Creates a problem statement that is related to a training request
- Identifies how the solution of the problem can be resolved by training

Supporting Attitudes

- Is willing to raise and distinguish training needs from non-training issues

Role: Course Designer

Advanced ### Advanced Planning Competency 9: Identifies the Training Issue and How It Relates to a Business Need

Organizational issues and business needs are explored, training issues extracted and documented. A training plan is written that provides solutions to the problems.

Results or Output

Training plan

Supporting Knowledge

- Is aware of business needs and their origins
- Is aware of the difference between issues, problems, and needs
- Is aware of the difference between symptoms and problems

Supporting Skills

- Creates a problem statement that is related to a business need
- Identifies a variety of solutions to the problem
- Only recommends a training solution when the problem can be appropriately resolved by training
- Identifies non-training problems and recommends alternative solutions

Supporting Attitudes

- Is willing to raise and distinguish training needs from non-training issues
- Is interested in the deeper or root causes of issues or problems

Role: Course Designer

Basic Planning Competency 10: States the Outcome, Results, and Objectives of the Training

Given a training issue, identifies whether the requested training is justified by the rationale from the person who requests the training.

Results or Output

Training event rationale

Supporting Knowledge

- Is aware of how to justify training needs
- Is aware of the desired results that could come from training solutions

Supporting Skills

- Uses specific, descriptive language to justify the requested training event
- Writes objectives for training request

Supporting Attitude

- Is helpful

Role: Course Designer

Advanced ### Advanced Planning Competency 10: States the Outcome, Results, and Objectives of the Training

Given a training issue that is related to a business need, identifies the desired outcome or results and the objective of the training to meet the business need.

Results or Output

Training plan

Supporting Knowledge

- Is aware of business needs and their origins

- Is aware of the desired results that could come from training solutions

Supporting Skills

- Uses specific, descriptive language to identify the desired outcome or results

- Writes objectives for training that will meet a business need

Supporting Attitude

- Is willing to adapt a focus for a project beyond a training component

Role: Course Designer

Basic Planning Competency 11: States the Performance Deficiency and Its Causes

Identifies the performance deficiency and its causes that are related to the proposed training event.

Results or Output

Training event justification

Supporting Knowledge

- Understands what causes performance deficiencies
- Understands how to fix performance deficiencies

Supporting Skills

- Describes performance deficiencies in an objective manner
- Describes the various types of causes for performance deficiencies

Supporting Attitudes

- Is open-minded
- Is objective

Role: Course Designer

Advanced

Advanced Planning Competency 11: States the Performance Deficiency and Its Causes

Identifies the performance deficiency and its causes that are related to the business need and the proposed training.

Results or Output

Performance deficiencies and causes

Supporting Knowledge

- Is aware of how the business works

- Understands what causes performance deficiencies

- Understands how to fix performance deficiencies

Supporting Skills

- Describes performance deficiencies in an objective manner

- Describes the various types of causes for performance deficiencies

Supporting Attitudes

- Is open-minded

- Is objective

- Is interested in the deeper or root causes of issues or problems

Role: Course Designer

Basic Planning Competency 12: Identifies or Establishes Performance Standards

Identifies existing performance standards for tasks that are performed deficiently. Where no standards exist, the course designer requests that the operations supervisor or manager establish performance standards.

Results or Output

Performance standards

Supporting Knowledge

- Is aware of existing performance standards
- Is aware of lines of authority for establishing performance standards

Supporting Skills

- Cites existing standards that are not being met by how the job is done currently
- If no standards exist, requests that the operations supervisor or manager establish performance standards

Supporting Attitudes

- Is flexible
- Is determined to develop a useful work product, given an approved format

Role: Course Designer

Advanced

Advanced Planning Competency 12: Identifies or Establishes Performance Standards

Identify existing performance standards for tasks that are performed deficiently. Where no standards exist, collaborates with subject-matter experts to establish performance standards.

Results or Output

Performance standards

Supporting Knowledge

- Is aware of existing performance standards
- Understands how to collaboratively establish performance standards

Supporting Skills

- Cites existing standards that are not being met by how the job is done currently
- If no standards exist, collaborates with subject-matter experts to establish performance standards in an approved format

Supporting Attitudes

- Is flexible
- Is determined to develop a useful work product, given an approved format

Role: Course Designer

Basic Planning Competency 13: Identifies the Target Population

Based on prior analysis, identifies the target population for this training project.

Results or Output

Target population statement

Supporting Knowledge

- Is aware of which people/employees constitute the target population
- Understands some of the decisions that will be made based on the data collected

Supporting Skills

- Asks appropriate questions
- Interviews a sufficient number of the target population to make appropriate recommendations
- Recommends content and grouping of the target population for the training

Supporting Attitudes

- Is sensitive to the needs of the target population

Role: Course Designer

Advanced △

Advanced Planning Competency 13: Identifies the Target Population

Based on prior analysis, identifies the target population for this training project.

Results or Output

Target population statement

Supporting Knowledge

- Is aware of which people/employees constitute the target population
- Is aware of different types of information to seek about the target population
- Understands the decisions that will be made based on the data collected
- Understands what constitutes appropriate questions for a specific target population

Supporting Skills

- Asks appropriate questions
- Interviews a sufficient number of the target population to make appropriate recommendations
- Collects information through surveys when appropriate
- Writes justifications for content selection and grouping decisions based on the data

Supporting Attitudes

- Is sensitive to the needs of the target population
- Avoids making the target population defensive and is willing to answer questions

Role: Course Designer

Basic Planning Competency 14: Establishes Criteria to Evaluate the Training

Identifies how the participant reaction and learning will be evaluated.

Results or Output

Evaluation tools

Supporting Knowledge

- Is aware of the reaction sheets
- Is aware of testing methods

Supporting Skills

- Identifies how to customize the reaction sheet for this training event
- Identifies ways to measure participant learning

Supporting Attitude

- Fairness in testing

Role: Course Designer

Advanced ***Advanced Planning Competency 14: Establishes Criteria to Evaluate the Training***

Identifies and gains agreement from the target population's manager for how the training project will be evaluated and which of the four levels of evaluation are appropriate for this project.

Results or Output

Evaluation tools

Supporting Knowledge

- Is aware of the four levels of evaluation

Supporting Skills

- Selects the appropriate levels of evaluation for this project

Supporting Attitude

- Flexibility

Role: Course Designer

Basic Planning Competency 15: Describes the Proposed Intervention

Describes the training event that will meet the need in the training plan objectives.

Results or Output

Training event description

Supporting Knowledge

- Understands what makes training effective
- Understands the cause-and-effect relationship of sequencing training activities

Supporting Skills

- Creates a content outline and learning objectives
- Describes the rationale for the sequence of training activities

Supporting Attitude

- Is interested in influencing the client

Role: Course Designer

Advanced ***Advanced Planning Competency 15: Describes the Proposed Intervention***
Describes the variety of activities in the appropriate sequence to address the
need in the training plan objectives.

Results or Output

Variety of activities and interventions, job aids

Supporting Knowledge

- Understands which types of activities are suited to specific objectives
- Understands the cause-and-effect relationship of sequencing project
  activities

Supporting Skills

- Lists the proposed activities (training, job aids, coaching, new policy,
  and so forth) for the project
- Describes the rationale for the sequence of activities

Supporting Attitude

- Is willing to provide enough detail to make the intervention
  understood

Role: Course Designer

Basic Planning Competency 16: Estimates the Cost of the Training Plan

Lists the anticipated expenses to conduct the training event.

Results or Output

Estimated costs

Supporting Knowledge

- Understands cost-collection techniques

Supporting Skills

- Estimates training expenses to design and present the training event

Supporting Attitudes

- Is willing to reveal true costs

Role: Course Designer

Advanced

Advanced Planning Competency 16: Estimates the Cost of the Training Plan

Lists the direct and indirect expenses to implement the training plan. Describes the cost of current performance. Compares current performance cost with the estimated cost of doing the training.

Results or Output

Feasibility cost estimate

Supporting Knowledge

- Understands cost estimation
- Understands methods of cost comparison

Supporting Skills

- Shows the cost of current performance, the cost of an implemented training plan, and when to expect a return on the training investment
- Distinguishes between direct and indirect expenses

Supporting Attitude

- Is willing to reveal true costs

Role: Course Designer

Basic Planning Competency 17: Builds a Partnership with Management to Ensure Success of the Training Plan

Creates and delivers to supervisors and managers an announcement of the training event, along with a description of the course content and learning objectives.

Results or Output

Training announcement

Supporting Knowledge

- Understands effective course announcements

Supporting Skills

- Produces a course announcement in a timely manner

Supporting Attitude

- Desires clarity and accuracy of course announcement

Role: Course Designer

Advanced Planning Competency 17: Builds a Partnership with Management to Ensure Success of the Training Plan

Partners with supervisors, managers, and learners before, during, and after the proposed training plan is carried out.

Results or Output

Partnership roles

Supporting Knowledge

- Is aware of appropriate partnership strategies for each phase of the project
- Understands the role of self and others in partnering on a training project

Supporting Skills

- Develops a partnership plan to gain the support of management and the target population for the training project
- Produces information and materials to support the training project

Supporting Attitude

- Is willing to go beyond the presentation of a training event to make a training project successful

Role: Course Designer

Basic Planning Competency 18: Schedules Training

Proposes a training schedule to attract maximum attendance from the target population.

Results or Output

Training schedule

Supporting Knowledge

- Is aware of organization's holidays

- Is aware of trainers' expertise in recommending trainers to teach classes

Supporting Skills

- Sets an optimum schedule of training classes according to trainer availability

- Resolves scheduling conflicts for trainers

Supporting Attitude

- Is willing to negotiate with trainers to create an optimum schedule

Role: Course Designer

Advanced *Advanced Planning Competency 18: Schedules Training*

Proposes a training schedule to attract maximum attendance from the target population. Resolves conflicts between the training schedule and the needs of the business.

Results or Output

Training schedule

Supporting Knowledge

- Understands how a training schedule can impact business needs
- Is aware of organization's holidays
- Is aware of trainers' expertise in recommending trainers to teach classes

Supporting Skills

- Sets an optimum schedule of training classes
- Resolves scheduling conflicts

Supporting Attitude

- Is willing to negotiate with trainers, supervisors, and trainees to create an optimum schedule

Role: Course Designer

Basic **Basic Development Competency 19: Creates a Broad Content Outline**
Using content experts and resources, creates a content outline that will allow participants to meet the course learning objectives.

Results or Output

Content outline

Supporting Knowledge

- Is aware of resources
- Knows how to research content topics

Supporting Skills

- Creates a broad content outline that contains enough detail to meet learning objectives but not so vague that developing materials is difficult

Supporting Attitude

- Openness to new ideas and revisions of the content outline

Role: Course Designer

Advanced
Advanced Development Competency 19: Creates a Broad Content Outline

Using content experts and resources, creates a content outline that will allow participants to meet the course learning objectives.

Results or Output

Content outline

Supporting Knowledge

- Is aware of resources
- Knows how to research content topics

Supporting Skills

- Creates a broad content outline that contains enough detail to meet learning objectives but not so vague that developing materials is difficult
- Filters content from various resources by focusing on learning objectives

Supporting Attitude

- Openness to new ideas and revisions of the content outline

Role: Course Designer

Basic Development Competency 20: Identifies Sources for Course Content

Identifies a variety of internal and external resources to provide enough detail for course content.

Results or Output

Resources

Supporting Knowledge

- Is aware of resources
- Knows how to research content topics

Supporting Skills

- Filters content from various resources by focusing on learning objectives

Supporting Attitude

- Openness to new ideas and revisions of the content outline

Role: Course Designer

Advanced ### *Advanced Development Competency 20: Identifies Sources for Course Content*

Identifies a variety of internal and external resources to provide enough detail for course content.

Results or Output

Resources

Supporting Knowledge

- Is aware of resources
- Knows how to research content topics

Supporting Skills

- Filters content from various resources by focusing on learning objectives
- Assures consistency of content selected
- Sequences content logically to meet the needs of the target population

Supporting Attitude

- Is open to new ideas and revisions of the content outline

Role: Course Designer

Basic Development Competency 21: Selects Appropriate Methods

Identifies appropriate training methods or combination of methods that will meet the objective.

Results or Output

Methods

Supporting Knowledge

- Is aware of a variety of training methods

Supporting Skills

- Selects appropriate learning methods to make delivery interesting to the learner
- Selects familiar and often-used learning methods

Supporting Attitude

- Is interested in avoiding boring training

Role: Course Designer

Advanced

Advanced Development Competency 21: Selects Appropriate Methods

Based on whether a learning objective focuses on achieving improved knowledge, skills, or attitudes, identifies appropriate training methods or combination of methods that will meet the objective.

Results or Output

Methods based on knowledge, skill, or attitudinal objectives

Supporting Knowledge

- Is aware of a variety of training methods
- Understands what type of training methods are best used to reach a particular learning objective

Supporting Skills

- Selects appropriate training methods that are related to the learning objective
- Avoids using training activities or methods merely for the sake of variety
- Selects a variety of training methods that appeal to different learning styles

Supporting Attitude

- Is willing to try new methods to enhance learning

Role: Course Designer

 Basic Development Competency 22: Sequences Training Methods
Given selected training methods, intuitively sequences the training methods according to past practices.

Results or Output

Sequenced training methods

Supporting Knowledge

- Is aware of how the organization's prior course content and training methods have been sequenced

Supporting Skills

- Sequences training methods to match past practices

Supporting Attitude

- Is consistent

Role: Course Designer

Advanced

Advanced Development Competency 22: Sequences Training Methods

Given selected training methods, sequences the methods according to the type of learning objective (knowledge or skill) and the experience, prior training, and motivation of the learner.

Results or Output

Sequenced training methods

Supporting Knowledge

- Is aware of the impact of the target population's experience, prior training, and motivation on sequencing training methods

- Is aware of the impact of knowledge objectives or skills objectives in sequencing training methods

- Is aware that a sequence of methods can be altered by an instructor, based on the immediate learning needs of a specific group from the target population

Supporting Skills

- Sequences training methods to suit the target population's experience, prior training, and motivation

- Explains to the trainer the logic for the sequence of training methods and how to make a transition from one training methods to the next

Supporting Attitudes

- Is willing to build sequencing options into a lesson plan

- Is willing to share the logic of the sequence with the trainer and the learner

Role: Course Designer

Basic **Basic Development Competency 23: Ensures a Variety of Pacing for Training Methods**

Assures a variety of training methods are used throughout a course.

Results or Output

Variety of training methods

Supporting Knowledge

- Is aware of a learner's need for a variety of training methods

Supporting Skills

- Assures a variety of training methods

Supporting Attitude

- Is interested in variety of training methods for its own sake

Role: Course Designer

Advanced

Advanced Development Competency 23: Ensures a Variety of Pacing for Training Methods

Assesses methods to ensure what the learner does change intensity at least every fifteen minutes. Assures a variety of training methods are used throughout a course.

Results or Output

Pacing plan

Supporting Knowledge

- Understands an adult learner's attention span
- Is aware of how to use a variety of training methods to improve retention

Supporting Skills

- Limits the use of any training method to a maximum of fifteen-minute increments
- Inserts active training methods, such as small group discussions, demonstrations, or simulations, once to twice per hour to prolong learner participation, learning, and retention

Supporting Attitudes

- Is willing to alter the design of a training program to increase the level of learner participation
- Uses techniques to involve the learners that help reach an objective, not just for the sake of activity

Role: Course Designer

 Basic Development Competency 24: Identifies How Much Practice Is Required to Learn a New Skill

Creates practice exercises for the target population to develop a skill.

Results or Output

Practice exercises

Supporting Knowledge

- Is aware of the need to practice a skill during training

Supporting Skills

- Creates skill practice exercises so the learner successfully develops a skill to complete the new task

Supporting Attitude

- Is accurate

Role: Course Designer

 Advanced

Advanced Development Competency 24: Identifies How Much Practice Is Required to Learn a New Skill

Assess the difficulty of doing a task once learned; assess the importance of doing a task in a standardized manner; and assess the frequency with which the task will be done on the job. Based on difficulty, importance, and frequency, use a decision tree to recommend whether a task can be taught successfully through a demonstration, basic training, or advanced training with multiple practice sessions and job aids.

Results or Output

Practice plan

Supporting Knowledge

- Understands the relationship of practicing a task during a training program and how and when the task is used on the job

- Understands task difficulty from the subject-matter expert's point of view

- Understands the need to do a task in a standardized manner

- Is aware of the frequency with which a task is done on the job

Supporting Skills

- Selects the appropriate amount of practice to successfully learn a new task

- Creates skill practice exercises so the learner successfully develops a skill to complete the new task

- Creates job aids to reinforce tasks that require advanced training

Supporting Attitude

- Is accurate

Role: Course Designer

Basic Development Competency 25: Writes Training Activities

Creates a variety of training activities to meet specific learning objectives.

Results or Output

Written activities

Supporting Knowledge

- Is aware of how to write different training activities

Supporting Skills

- Creates learning activities such as lectures, skill practice exercises, and discussions to meet the learning objectives

- Selects learning activities developed by others to enhance learning activities

- Develops handout materials

- Develops visual aids

Supporting Attitude

- Shows enthusiasm for different types of learning activities

Role: Course Designer

Advanced

Advanced Development Competency 25: Writes Training Activities

Creates a variety of training activities to meet specific learning objectives.

Results or Output

Written activities

Supporting Knowledge

- Is aware of which type of activity can best accomplish a learning objective
- Is aware of different formats for learning activities
- Understands how different activities promote learner participation

Supporting Skills

- Identifies the best learning experience and crafts an appropriate activity that can best accomplish a learning objective
- Creates learning activities such as lectures, skill practice exercises, discussions, case studies, simulations, and games to meet the learning objectives
- Customizes learning activities developed by others to enhance learning activities
- Writes questions for the instructor to facilitate each learning activity and promote discovery learning
- Develops handout materials
- Develops visual aids

Supporting Attitudes

- Shows enthusiasm for different types of learning activities
- Shows determination to completely develop instructions and transitions to facilitate learning activities

---

Role: Course Designer

Basic Development Competency 26: Identifies the Appropriate Type of Lesson Plan for a Specific Course

Selects the lesson plan format commonly used in the organization.

Results or Output

Template for lesson plan

Supporting Knowledge

- Is aware of types of lesson plans previously used in the organization

Supporting Skills

- Selects a lesson plan format

Supporting Attitude

- Is consistent

Role: Course Designer

Advanced Development Competency 26: Identifies the Appropriate Type of Lesson Plan for a Specific Course

Given an assessment and three types of lesson plan formats, selects the appropriate type of format for a specific course.

Results or Output

Template for lesson plan

Supporting Knowledge

- Is aware of different types of lesson plans
- Understands factors that influence selection of a specific lesson plan format

Supporting Skills

- Selects an appropriate lesson plan format

Supporting Attitude

- Is willing to consider all the factors influencing decision making

Role: Course Designer

Basic Development Competency 27: Writes the Lesson Plan

Writes a lesson plan that includes necessary information for the successful presentation of a course.

Results or Output

Lesson plan

Supporting Knowledge

- Is aware of all the parts required in a lesson plan

Supporting Skills

- Writes a lesson plan with enough detail for the successful presentation of a course

Supporting Attitude

- Is willing to provide enough information to make the lesson plan complete and useful

Role: Course Designer

Advanced **Advanced Development Competency 27: Writes the Lesson Plan**

Writes a lesson plan that includes necessary information for the successful presentation of a course.

Results or Output

Lesson plan

Supporting Knowledge

- Understands all the parts required in a lesson plan
- Is aware of the training skills of the instructor for whom the lesson plan is written

Supporting Skills

- Writes a lesson plan with enough detail for the successful presentation of a course
- Writes supporting instructor notes where appropriate
- Writes information for the instructor to transition from one activity to the next
- Writes additional facilitator processing questions for each activity that will help the instructor customize a presentation of the course for specific target populations

Supporting Attitude

- Is willing to provide enough information to make the lesson plan complete and useful

Role: Course Designer

Basic Development Competency 28: Conducts a Pilot Workshop and Makes Appropriate Revisions

Partners with trainers to conduct a pilot workshop of a new course that includes representatives from the target population. Makes appropriate revisions based on feedback from pilot participants.

Results or Output

Pilot workshop, course revisions

Supporting Knowledge

- Is aware of the need to pilot workshop for a new course

Supporting Skills

- Invites representatives of the target population
- Solicits feedback from pilot workshop participants
- Makes appropriate changes in course materials

Supporting Attitudes

- Is willing to hear all opinions
- Is willing to make needed revisions

Role: Course Designer

Advanced

Advanced Development Competency 28: Conducts a Pilot Workshop and Makes Appropriate Revisions

Partners with trainers to conduct a pilot workshop of a new course that includes representatives from the target population, subject-matter experts, management, and other course designers and trainers. Makes appropriate revisions based on feedback from pilot participants.

Results or Output

Pilot workshop, course revisions

Supporting Knowledge

- Is aware of who should attend a pilot workshop for a new course
- Is aware of biases of each constituent group

Supporting Skills

- Invites representatives of different constituent groups
- Solicits feedback from pilot workshop participants
- Makes appropriate changes in course materials

Supporting Attitudes

- Is willing to hear all opinions
- Is willing to make needed revisions

Role: Course Designer

Basic Evaluation Competency 29: Designs a Reaction Sheet to Get Feedback from Participants

Makes revisions to the standard reaction sheet to solicit appropriate feedback from course participants.

Results or Output

Reaction sheet

Supporting Knowledge

- Is aware of the types of feedback that are helpful to the course developer, instructor, and management

Supporting Skills

- Customizes questions from the standard feedback form that solicits information regarding the usefulness of the content and the effectiveness of the instructor

- Selects a variety of objective questions and short-answer narrative questions

- Uses a format that is familiar to learners

Supporting Attitude

- Is interested in learner reaction to the course

Role: Course Designer

Advanced **Advanced Evaluation Competency 29: Designs a Reaction Sheet to Get Feedback from Participants**

Creates a reaction sheet to solicit appropriate feedback from course participants.

Results or Output

Reaction sheet

Supporting Knowledge

- Is aware of the types of feedback that are helpful to the course developer, instructor, and management
- Is aware of how to construct feedback questions to avoid bias

Supporting Skills

- Writes appropriate questions that solicit information regarding the usefulness of the content, effectiveness of the instructor, and demographic information
- Selects a variety of objective questions and short-answer narrative questions
- Uses a format that allows for easy summary of data into a trend analysis
- Creates an online version of the feedback form

Supporting Attitude

- Is willing to write a bias-free reaction sheet

Role: Course Designer

Basic Evaluation Competency 30: Writes a Test to Measure Learning

Based on the course learning objectives, writes objective and subjective tests that measure learning and skill development.

Results or Output

Test

Supporting Knowledge

- Is aware of what type of questions are appropriate to measure knowledge and skills

- Understands how to write test questions that measure the learning objectives

Supporting Skills

- Selects course subject matter that is to be tested as part of the end-of-course evaluation

- Writes appropriate test questions

Supporting Attitudes

- Is fair and impartial

Role: Course Designer

Advanced **Advanced Evaluation Competency 30: Writes a Test to Measure Learning**
Based on the course learning objectives, writes valid and reliable objective and subjective tests that measure learning and skill development.

Results or Output

Valid and reliable test

Supporting Knowledge

- Understands what constitutes a reliable and valid test
- Is aware of what type of questions are appropriate to measure knowledge and skills
- Understands how to write test questions that measure the learning objectives

Supporting Skills

- Selects course subject matter that is to be tested as part of the end-of-course evaluation
- Writes appropriate test questions
- Assures the test is valid and reliable

Supporting Attitudes

- Is fair and impartial

Role: Course Designer

Basic Evaluation Competency 31: Creates a Skill Performance Checklist to Measure the Transfer of Learning to the Workplace

Creates a skill performance checklist for use by a trainer at the end of the course to assess skill development during training. A supervisor can use the checklist to measure whether new skills learned in the course are being used on the job.

Results or Output

Skill performance checklist

Supporting Knowledge

- Understands how to write a skill performance checklist based on a learning objective and task analysis

Supporting Skills

- Creates a skill performance checklist
- Uses a skill performance checklist to identify skill development during training

Supporting Attitude

- Is fair

Role: Course Designer

 Advanced **Advanced Evaluation Competency 31: Creates a Skill Performance Checklist to Measure the Transfer of Learning to the Workplace**

Creates a skill performance checklist for use by a trainer at the end of the course to assess skill development during training. A supervisor can use the checklist to measure whether new skills learned in the course are being used on the job.

Results or Output

Skill performance checklist

Supporting Knowledge

- Understands how to write a skill performance checklist based on a learning objective and task analysis
- Understands how to validate a skill performance checklist

Supporting Skills

- Creates a skill performance checklist
- Validates a skill performance checklist
- Uses a skill performance checklist to document skill development to meet personnel and regulatory requirements

Supporting Attitudes

- Is fair
- Uses discipline to follow a process to properly document skill development

Role: Course Designer

Basic Evaluation Competency 32: Creates a Return on Investment Analysis to Identify Results

Collects information that could be used to identify the results of a training course.

Results or Output

Collected cost information

Supporting Knowledge

- Is aware of what data to collect

Supporting Skills

- Collects cost information
- Collects data that demonstrates a benefit was achieved from conducting a course

Supporting Attitude

- Shows concern for accuracy

Role: Course Designer

Advanced **Advanced Evaluation Competency 32: Creates a Return on Investment Analysis to Identify Results**

Measures the results of a training course by conducting a return on investment analysis.

Results or Output

Analysis

Supporting Knowledge

- Is aware of different types of analysis and data collection needed to demonstrate a return on investment

- Understands analysis techniques

Supporting Skills

- Collects cost information

- Collects data that demonstrates a benefit was achieved from conducting a course

- Analyzes data

- Presents data in a convincing manner

- Responds to technical questions

Supporting Attitude

- Shows concern for accuracy

Course Designer Development Plan

Following the completion of a competency checklist, create a development plan that identifies the course designer's strengths, identifies areas for coaching and feedback, and identifies missing knowledge and skills, along with resources for development. Beginning a development plan with a course designer's strengths acknowledges what this person has that can be built on for further development. Strengths can also be used to mentor others. Areas for coaching and feedback can be competencies that were not observed. They may be competencies that require more practice because the course designer may already have supporting knowledge and attitudes, but did not display the skill. Areas can be deficient because some knowledge, skills, or attitudes are missing. Refer to the secondary checklists to identify what is missing and to plan what resources are available to build these competencies.

Gain agreement from management for the commitment of resources for development. Agree on a time frame for the development and re-evaluation of the competency.

A sample Course Designer Development Plan Template is on the next page

Course Designer Development Plan Template

Course Designer's Name: _____ Date: _____

1. List competencies that exceed expectation:

2. Identify

Underdeveloped or unobserved competencies	Knowledge, skills, and attitudes to acquire

3. Identify competencies that require coaching and feedback:

4. Identify resources required to develop these competencies:

Target date for re-evaluation:

_____

Training Manager Competencies

Chapter Objectives

- To identify strategic competencies for those who manage a training function
- To identify tactical competencies for those who manage a training function
- To identify why these competencies are needed

Chapter Tools

- Competency Model Checklist for Training Managers
- Expanded Competency Checklists for Training Managers
- Training Manager Development Plan Template

Assessment Questions

- What are the competencies for training managers?
- How can these competencies be measured?
- Which competencies apply to my role as a training manager?

Competencies Required of a Training Manager

Training managers are responsible for the overall working of a training function. Competencies required for an effective training function are both *strategic* and *tactical.* Strategic competencies include planning, organizing, staffing, and budgeting. Tactical competencies include controlling training and development (T&D) operations or T&D projects. Frequently, the training manager uses tactical competencies when acting as an internal performance consultant to link T&D operations with other organization units. Many training managers in large organizations present management development training for the executive group. It might be useful for training managers who conduct training to review the competencies listed in Chapter 3. Many training managers have additional responsibilities and need other competencies, such as marketing the training function, which are listed for the training coordinator role in Chapter 7.

A variety of titles for the role of a training manager include some of these emerging titles: chief learning officer, learning compliance officer, performance consultant, internal consultant, training supervisor, or coach and mentor to newer department members.

Strategic Competencies

An organization's mission, vision, and operation drive the use of strategic competencies for training managers. Planning for the training function is successful when it is tied to an organization's strategic plan. The training manager who follows the plan can then successfully organize the training function, organize internal and external resources appropriately, budget for the function to reach its objectives, and appropriately staff the function.

Tactical Competencies

In addition to strategic competencies, the training manager needs additional competencies, such as project management and internal performance consulting competencies.

Competency Checklists for the Training Manager

Following are two checklists that outline and define broad strategic and tactical competencies for the training manager. When compiled they become a competency model for the training manager.

All the competencies together describe the optimum behaviors for a training manager. Use the checklists to assess whether a training manager does the tasks described. Ratings of "A" and "B" are suggested to distinguish whether the competency is held at the "advanced" or "basic" level. For either an "A" or "B" rating, tangible results or outputs are visible. A rating of "I" stands for "incomplete" because tangible results or output are not observed, are missing, or are partially complete. Remember, a competency is either observed or not observed.

Following the Training Manager Competency Model Checklist is a second pair of checklists. The first expands on the numbered training manager competencies and provides a description of the *basic* competency along with supporting knowledge, skills, and attitudes. Results or output for each competency are also provided. Another checklist is provided with *advanced* competency descriptions with supporting knowledge, skills, and attitudes. At the end of the Competency Model Checklist, the rater shows the total percentage of competencies observed. Remember to decide prior to the observation what percentage of competencies must be present to show competence. See Chapter 9 for information about using competencies as part of a certification process.

How to Use the Competency Checklists

Use competency checklists to rate yourself or as part of a collaborative process when being rated by another person. To customize the training manager competency model, first review all the checklists. Next, select those competencies that are either required or desirable for the training manager role in your organization. Download the desired checklists from the CD that accompanies this book to create a customized checklist. Either eliminate the competencies that do not apply or rate the competency as N/A for "not applicable." Prior to assessing a competency, agree with the rater on the meaning of the competencies. Review the expanded descriptions with supporting knowledge, skills, and attitudes to determine *basic* versus *advanced* levels of competency. Also, when rating another person, ensure a shared definition of each competency and what level of competency is being assessed. See the resource section at the end of this book for sample completed assessments and development plans.

Competency Model Checklist for Training Managers

A = meets *advanced* competency (advanced tangible results or outputs are visible)

B = meets *basic* competency (tangible results or outputs are visible)

I = *incomplete* (tangible results or outputs are not observed, missing or partially complete)

N = behavior *not* observed (not competent)

Rating	Training Manager Competency	Basic Results or Output	Advanced Results or Output
	Planning Competencies		
	1. Conducts long-term planning and anticipates future training needs	Written business plan	Written business plan
	2. Links training function activity to vision, mission, and business plan	Internal training function adjustments	Written vision Written mission
	3. Ensures legal, ethical, and regulatory compliance	Compliance reports	Written ethics policy Compliance reports
	Organizing Competency		
	4. Assures the training function is organized for optimum results	Organization chart	Organization chart, reorganization plans, if needed
	Staffing Competencies		
	5. Selects internal trainers systematically	Internal trainer criteria to assess subject-matter expertise and practical expertise	Internal trainer criteria to assess subject-matter expertise, training skills, and practical expertise
	6. Gives internal trainers feedback	Participant feedback form for trainers Direct observation notes	Participant feedback form for trainers Trend analysis report of ratings from classes taught by the trainers Coaching of trainers based on feedback data and observations Participant test results

Rating	Training Manager Competency	Basic Results or Output	Advanced Results or Output
	7. Develops internal trainer skills	Professional development events	Professional development plan for individual trainers and the department
	8. Provides access to training management	Project plans Planning meeting minutes	Project plans Planning meeting minutes
	9. Promotes a training management relationship to trainers, course developers	Letters of recognition	Letters of recognition Public recognition
	10. Supports and develops staff	Line item in budget Regularly scheduled individual and staff meetings	Line item in budget
	11. Participates in outside professional organizations Conference presentation materials	Receipts for membership dues Conference presentation materials	Receipts for membership dues
	12. Keeps up-to-date with training trends	Trend reports	Trend reports New training materials
	13. Uses and supervises external resources Contracts with external resources and forms Budget	Written proposals for review Written proposal review process Contracts with external resources Budget	Requests for proposals
Budgeting Competencies			
	14. Prepares a budget	Proposed budget	Proposed budget
	15. Monitors a budget	Budget reports	Budget reports
	16. Modifies a budget budget modifications	Training proposals, budget modifications	Training proposals,

Rating	Training Manager Competency	Basic Results or Output	Advanced Results or Output
	Project Management Competencies		
	17. Assesses the need to create a project team	Project plan Project team	Project plan Project team Project report
	18. Uses project management tools appropriately	Project plan changes Project reports	Project plan changes Project reports
	19. Ends projects appropriately	Final project report	Final project report
	Internal Consulting Competencies		
	20. Acts as an internal consultant to the client	Training department activity reports	Uses a consulting process Consulting plan Department activity reports
	21. Selects the appropriate role for each situation	Agreed-on outcomes	Agreed-on outcomes
	22. Uses a systematic internal consulting process	Needs assessment data Training program	Needs assessment data Training program Performance improvement plan Measurable results from an intervention
	% Total of competencies observed		
	% Total required for competence		

Expanded Competency Checklist for the Training Manager

Role: Training Manager

Basic Planning Competency 1: Conducts Long-Term Planning and Anticipates Future Training Needs

The training function is given funding based on a business plan.

Results or Output

Written business plan

Supporting Knowledge

- Is aware of the organization's long-term and short-term business plans
- Is aware of training requirements

Supporting Skills

- Creates a training plan based on future organizational needs

Supporting Attitude

- Deals fairly with others in internal relationships

Role: Training Manager

 Advanced

Advanced Planning Competency 1: Conducts Long-Term Planning and Anticipates Future Training Needs

The training function has management support by providing time, funding, training, and facilities to continually improve internal processes. The training manager locates and recognizes internal and external training talent.

Results or Output

Written business plan

Supporting Knowledge

- Is aware of resource requirements in the organization's long-term and short-term business plans
- Is aware of funding sources
- Is aware of training requirements
- Is aware of facility requirements
- Is aware of training talent

Supporting Skills

- Creates a training plan based on future organizational needs
- Develops relationships for funding and facility sources

Supporting Attitudes

- Is fair and impartial
- Is open to developing relationships
- Deals fairly with resource suppliers

Role: Training Manager

Basic Planning Competency 2: Links Training Function Activity to Vision, Mission, and Business Plan

A training plan is adjusted, when necessary, to the organization's vision, mission, and objectives.

Results or Output

Internal training function adjustments

Supporting Knowledge

- Is aware of appropriate content for vision and mission statements
- Is aware of business objectives

Supporting Skills

- Adjusts internal training functions
- Compiles information from internal and external resources

Supporting Attitudes

- Promotes collaboration with internal and external sources
- Supports varying points of view

Role: Training Manager

Advanced

Advanced Planning Competency 2: Links Training Function to Vision, Mission, and Business Plan

When necessary, the vision, mission, and objectives are adjusted based on internal and external information from executive management, trainers, and the client.

Results or Output

Written vision and mission statements for the training function

Supporting Knowledge

- Is aware of appropriate content for vision and mission statements
- Is aware of business objective
- Is aware of sources for internal and external information that contributes to vision, mission, and objectives

Supporting Skills

- Writes vision and mission statements for the training function
- Compiles information from internal and external resources
- Writes specific, measurable, and attainable time-bound objectives that relate to the organization's vision and mission

Supporting Attitudes

- Promotes collaboration with internal and external sources
- Supports varying points of view

Role: Training Manager

 Basic Planning Competency 3: Ensures Legal, Ethical, and Regulatory Compliance

As related to the training function, the training manager assures the function and its products and services comply with international, federal, state, and local laws and regulations.

Results or Output

Compliance reports

Supporting Knowledge

- Is aware of international, federal, state, and local legal requirements
- Is aware of international, federal, state, and local regulations

Supporting Skills

- Complies with reporting requirements accurately and in a timely manner
- Teaches others about compliance issues

Supporting Attitude

- Openness about compliance issues

Role: Training Manager

Advanced Planning Competency 3: Ensures Legal, Ethical, and Regulatory Compliance

As related to the training function, the training manager assures the function and its products and services comply with international, federal, state, and local laws and regulations. Ethical practices are modeled and encouraged in others.

Results or Output

Written ethics policy, compliance reports

Supporting Knowledge

- Is aware of international, federal, state, and local legal requirements
- Is aware of ethical issues
- Is aware of international, federal, state, and local regulations

Supporting Skills

- Complies with reporting requirements accurately and in a timely manner
- Teaches others about compliance issues
- Acts in an ethical manner and models it to others

Supporting Attitudes

- Encourages ethical behavior in others
- Talks openly about compliance issues

Role: Training Manager

Basic Organizing Competency 4: Assures the Training Function Is Organized for Optimum Results

The training function reports and works toward optimum results, whether as part of a line operation, support function, or independently organized.

Results or Output

Organization chart

Supporting Knowledge

- Is aware of the advantages and disadvantages of centralized and decentralized training functions
- Is aware of how line operations are organized

Supporting Skills

- Acts to take advantage of the strengths of the training function's organization
- Acts to overcome disadvantages of how the function is organized

Supporting Attitudes

- Shows eagerness to work toward a successful function, regardless of where the function reports

Role: Training Manager

Advanced

Advanced Organizing Competency 4: Assures the Training Function Is Organized for Optimum Results

Training function seeks to report where it can work toward optimum results. Whether as part of a line operation, support function, or independently organized, is assessed and modified as needed.

Results or Output

Organization chart, reorganization plans, if needed

Supporting Knowledge

- Is aware of the advantages and disadvantages of centralized and decentralized training functions
- Is aware of how line operations are organized

Supporting Skills

- Acts to take advantage of the strengths of the training function's organization
- Acts to overcome disadvantages of how the function is organized

Supporting Attitudes

- Is willing to renegotiate where the training function reports to overcome disadvantages
- Shows eagerness to work toward a successful function, regardless of where the function reports

Role: Training Manager

 Basic Staffing Competency 5: Selects Internal Trainers Systematically

The training function selects internal trainer candidates who demonstrate knowledge of subject matter and practical expertise in the field.

Results or Output

Internal trainer criteria to assess subject-matter expertise and practical expertise

Supporting Knowledge

- Is aware of staffing needs for the function
- Is aware of criteria for those who fill trainer positions

Supporting Skills

- Interviews candidates for training positions with appropriate questions
- Selects the best candidates for training positions by applying criteria objectively
- Assists trainers in relating learning to the organization's business needs

Supporting Attitudes

- Is able to be impartial and objective in the selection process
- Makes the selection process transparent and therefore fair

Role: Training Manager

Advanced
Advanced Staffing Competency 5: Selects Internal Trainers Systematically

The training function selects internal trainer candidates through a formal assessment process and requires candidates to demonstrate knowledge of subject matter, training skills, and practical expertise in the field. Additional demonstrated ability to relate learning and training to organizational business needs is required.

Results or Output

Internal trainer criteria to assess subject-matter expertise, training skills, and practical expertise

Supporting Knowledge

- Is aware of staffing needs for the function
- Is aware of criteria for those who fill trainer positions

Supporting Skills

- Selects the best candidates for training positions by applying criteria objectively
- Assists trainers in relating learning and training to the organization's business needs

Supporting Attitudes

- Is impartial and objective in the selection process
- Makes the selection process transparent and therefore fair

Role: Training Manager

Basic Staffing Competency 6: Gives Internal Trainers Feedback

Training managers use feedback from participants and their direct observations to develop internal trainers.

Results or Output

Feedback form for trainers, direct observation notes

Supporting Knowledge

- Is aware of how to give feedback to avoid making the trainer defensive
- Is aware of the existing performance review and development process

Supporting Skills

- Selects appropriate data from participant feedback as the basis for feedback to trainers
- Compiles appropriate feedback from personal observations
- Completes a performance review form
- Give developmental feedback to trainers

Supporting Attitudes

- Is impartial
- Is sensitive to the feelings of trainers

Role: Training Manager

Advanced Staffing Competency 6: Gives Internal Trainers Feedback

Advanced

Training managers use feedback from participants, trend analysis, direct observations, and skill test results from participants to develop internal trainers.

Results or Output

Feedback form for trainers, trend analysis report of ratings from classes taught by the trainers, direct observation comments, test results

Supporting Knowledge

- Is aware of how to give feedback to avoid making the trainer defensive
- Is aware of how trend analysis reveals a trainer's strengths and weaknesses
- Is aware of direct observation techniques

Supporting Skills

- Completes a trend analysis from raw data
- Selects appropriate data from trend reports as the basis for feedback to trainers
- Gives developmental feedback to trainers
- Compiles appropriate feedback from personal observations
- Reports test results that demonstrate skill improvement by participants

Supporting Attitudes

- Is impartial
- Is sensitive to the feelings of trainers

Role: Training Manager

Basic Staffing Competency 7: Develops Internal Trainer Skills

The professional development of internal trainers in terms of their knowledge of the subject matter, training, and practical experience in the field is a sporadic and intermittent element in the operation.

Results or Output

Professional development event

Supporting Knowledge

- Is aware of evaluation systems to improve trainer performance
- Understands the subject-matter expertise required by trainers
- Is aware of good instructional skills
- Is aware of the relationship between practical experience and its influence on successful training

Supporting Skills

- Presents events to develop subject-matter experts as trainers
- Coaches trainers in subject matter
- Coaches trainers in how to train
- Relates field experience to successful training

Supporting Attitudes

- Shows empathy toward those who are developing skills
- Is interested in the development of subordinates

Role: Training Manager

Advanced

Advanced Staffing Competency 7: Develops Internal Trainer Skills

The professional development of internal trainers in terms of their knowledge of the subject matter, training, and practical experience in the field is a regular element in the operation.

Results or Output

Professional development plan for individual trainers and for the department

Supporting Knowledge

- Is aware of evaluation systems to improve trainer performance
- Understands the subject-matter expertise required by trainers
- Is aware of good instructional skills
- Is aware of the relationship between practical experience and its influence on successful training

Supporting Skills

- Conducts regularly planned events to develop subject-matter experts as trainers
- Systematically coaches trainers in subject matter
- Systematically coaches trainers in how to train
- Relates field experience to successful training

Supporting Attitudes

- Shows empathy toward those who are developing skills
- Is interested in the development of subordinates

Role: Training Manager

Basic Staffing Competency 8: Provides Access to Training Management

The training manager gives direct access to subordinate trainers and supports their efforts.

Results or Output

Project plans, planning meeting minutes

Supporting Knowledge

- Is aware of the need for subordinates to have access to the training manager

Supporting Skills

- Creates project plans from subordinate input
- Sponsors and coaches subordinate trainers
- Facilitates input from subordinates during regularly scheduled staff meetings
- Responds to individual requests as needed

Supporting Attitudes

- Is willing to support subordinate trainers
- Is willing to be accessible to subordinate trainers

Role: Training Manager

 Advanced

Advanced Staffing Competency 8: Provides Access to Training Management

The training manager gives direct access to subordinate trainers and supports their efforts. Management participates as a sponsor of the training function.

Results or Output

Project plans, planning meeting minutes

Supporting Knowledge

- Is aware of the need for subordinates to have access to the training manager
- Understands how to maintain organization management support for the training function

Supporting Skills

- Creates project plans from subordinate input
- Sponsors and coaches subordinate trainers
- Facilitates input from subordinates during regularly scheduled staff meetings
- Maintains contact with organization management

Supporting Attitudes

- Is willing to support subordinate trainers
- Is willing to be accessible to subordinate trainers

Role: Training Manager

Basic Staffing Competency 9: Promotes Training Management Relationship to Trainers, Course Developers

Recognition and appreciation of individual and team contributions are normal and are consistently used for professional growth.

Results or Output

Letters of recognition

Supporting Knowledge

- Is aware of what constitutes a unique versus a normal contribution from subordinates
- Is aware of recognition channels in the organization

Supporting Skills

- Writes commendations for subordinates
- Gives praise and recognition privately

Supporting Attitudes

- Is interested in providing motivational recognition
- Is fair and consistent with subordinates

Role: Training Manager

Advanced

Advanced Staffing Competency 9: Promotes Training Management Relationship to Trainers, Course Developers

Recognition and appreciation of individual and team contributions are normal and publicly expressed and are consistently used for professional growth.

Results or Output

Letters of recognition, public recognition

Supporting Knowledge

- Is aware of what constitutes a unique versus a normal contribution from subordinates

- Is aware of recognition channels in the organization

Supporting Skills

- Writes commendations for subordinates

- Publicizes accomplishments of subordinates through recognition channels

- Gives praise appropriately

- Solicits recognition from management for the training function

- Uses multiple channels of recognition that appeal to the subordinate

Supporting Attitudes

- Is interested in providing motivational recognition

- Is fair and consistent with subordinates

Role: Training Manager

Basic Staffing Competency 10: Supports and Develops Staff

Personnel are given time and resources for their professional development.

Results or Output

Line item in budget

Supporting Knowledge

- Understands how to develop subordinates
- Is aware of resources available to develop subordinates

Supporting Skills

- Meets occasionally to develop subordinates
- Provides resources to develop subordinates
- Coaches subordinates

Supporting Attitudes

- Includes all subordinates in the development process
- Desires to improve the skills of subordinates

Role: Training Manager

Advanced

Advanced Staffing Competency 10: Supports and Develops Staff

Personnel are routinely given time, attention, and resources for their professional development.

Results or Output

Line item in budget, regularly scheduled individual and staff meetings

Supporting Knowledge

- Understands how to develop subordinates
- Is aware of career path in the organization
- Is aware of resources available to develop subordinates

Supporting Skills

- Meets routinely to develop subordinates
- Provides resources, including time, to develop subordinates
- Coaches subordinates

Supporting Attitudes

- Includes all subordinates in the development process
- Desires to improve the skills of subordinates

Role: Training Manager

Basic Staffing Competency 11: *Participates in Outside Professional Organizations*

Active membership in professional organizations is normal. Trainers attend presentations at professional conferences.

Results or Output

Receipts for membership dues, conference presentation materials

Supporting Knowledge

- Is aware of the role of professional organizations in developing self and subordinates
- Is aware of the need to keep up with training trends

Supporting Skills

- Is an active member of professional training organization(s)
- Attends presentations at professional training conferences

Supporting Attitude

- Values keeping self and subordinates up-to-date with training trends

Role: Training Manager

 Advanced *Advanced Staffing Competency 11: Participates in Outside Professional Organizations*

Active membership in professional organizations is normal. Trainers are trend setters among their peers, giving presentations at professional conferences.

Results or Output

Receipts for membership dues, conference presentation materials

Supporting Knowledge

- Is aware of the role of professional organizations in developing self and subordinates
- Is aware of the need to keep up with training trends

Supporting Skills

- Is an active member of professional training organization(s)
- Regularly reads professional training publications
- Gives presentations at professional training conferences
- Conducts research into best practices in the training field

Supporting Attitudes

- Is recognized by peers as a contributor to the training field
- Values keeping self and subordinates up-to-date with training trends

Role: Training Manager

Basic Staffing Competency 12: Keeps Up-to-Date with Training Trends

Training manager reviews trend updates and new research developments that affect training.

Results or Output

Trend reports

Supporting Knowledge

- Is aware of training trends and new research developments affecting training

Supporting Skills

- Shares trend updates and research information within the training function

Supporting Attitude

- Sees that change can be positive

Role: Training Manager

Advanced

Advanced Staffing Competency 12: Keeps Up-to-Date with Training Trends

The training manager shares trend updates and new research developments that affect training and encourages integration of new materials into training programs and how business is done.

Results or Output

Trend reports, new training materials

Supporting Knowledge

- Is aware of training trends and new research developments affecting training

- Is aware of how trends and new research developments can contribute to the organization's results

- Is aware of the impact of world and business events on the training function

Supporting Skills

- Uses trend update and research information to improve training programs

- Supports and coaches subordinates to integrate appropriate trends and research findings into training programs

Supporting Attitudes

- Believes change can be positive

- Thinks some trends and research can improve existing training programs

Role: Training Manager

Basic
Basic Staffing Competency 13: Uses and Supervises External Resources

The training function identifies the need for external resources and contracts with needed resources for desired services. External resources are monitored for results within budget.

Results or Output

Process review, contracts with external resources, budgets

Supporting Knowledge

- Understands how to evaluate proposals against objective criteria
- Understands elements required to monitor a budget

Supporting Skills

- Evaluates proposals against objective criteria
- Selects external resources based on need
- Monitors a budget

Supporting Attitude

- Values fairness and transparency when dealing with external resources

Role: Training Manager

Advanced

Advanced Staffing Competency 13: Uses and Supervises External Resources

The training function identifies the need for external resources, receives proposals, selects, and contracts with needed resources on a cost-effective basis for the best value. External resources are monitored for results within budget.

Results or Output

Requests for proposals, written proposal review process and forms, contracts with external resources, budget

Supporting Knowledge

- Knows how to write a request for proposal to include appropriate elements
- Understands how to evaluate proposals against objective criteria
- Understands elements required to monitor a budget

Supporting Skills

- Writes requests for proposal, including scope of work and contracting requirements
- Establishes an objective review process to review proposals fairly
- Evaluates proposals against objective criteria
- Selects external resources for the best value
- Monitors a budget
- Monitors external resources for contract compliance and to obtain full value

Supporting Attitude

- Values fairness and transparency when dealing with external resources

Role: Training Manager

Basic Budgeting Competency 14: Prepares a Budget

Given the constraints of the business, prepares a budget in a timely manner.

Results or Output

Proposed budget

Supporting Knowledge

- Understands the components of a training budget
- Understands the business constraints of the organization during the budgeting process

Supporting Skills

- Prepares a budget based on an appropriate increase/decrease from the prior budget period
- Submits a budget in a timely manner

Supporting Attitudes

- Values accuracy and timeliness

Role: Training Manager

Advanced **Advanced Budgeting Competency 14: Prepares a Budget**

Given the constraints of the business, prepares a budget in a timely manner and justifies requests beyond the norm.

Results or Output

Proposed budget

Supporting Knowledge

- Understands the components of a training budget
- Understands the business constraints of the organization during the budgeting process

Supporting Skills

- Reviews business and training plans to anticipate budget needs
- Completes needs assessments as appropriate
- Identifies proposed suppliers and creates estimates
- Submits justification for items requested that are above the norm
- Prepares a budget that takes increases/decreases into account
- Actively seeks methods to reduce costs
- Submits a budget in a timely manner

Supporting Attitude

- Values accuracy and timeliness

Role: Training Manager

Basic Budgeting Competency 15: Monitors a Budget

Tracks expenditures and reports on irregularities on a monthly or as-needed basis.

Results or Output

Budget reports

Supporting Knowledge

- Understands the importance of tracking a budget
- Is aware of techniques to monitor a budget

Supporting Skills

- Monitors a budget by tracking expenditures
- Reports irregularities on a monthly or as-needed basis

Supporting Attitude

- Values integrity and accuracy in budget oversight

Role: Training Manager

Advanced

Advanced Budgeting Competency 15: Monitors a Budget

Tracks expenditures and reports on irregularities on a monthly or as-needed basis.

Results or Output

Budget reports

Supporting Knowledge

- Understands the importance of tracking a budget
- Is aware of techniques to monitor a budget

Supporting Skills

- Monitors a budget by tracking expenditures
- Requires progress reports prior to approving expenditures
- Requires documentation and description of line item expenses
- Reports irregularities on a monthly or as-needed basis
- Creates return on investment reports for training events

Supporting Attitude

- Values integrity and accuracy in budget oversight

Role: Training Manager

Basic Budgeting Competency 16: Modifies a Budget

Given unforeseen circumstances, modifies or amends the budget based on a cost-effective proposal.

Results or Output

Training proposals, budget modifications

Supporting Knowledge

- Is aware of situations that call for a budget modification
- Understands the budget amendment process

Supporting Skills

- Selects appropriate options for budget modification requests
- Develops justifications for requests to amend the budget

Supporting Attitudes

- Is flexible and willing to modify the budget when unforeseen circumstances arise

Role: Training Manager

Advanced Budgeting Competency 16: Modifies a Budget

Given unforeseen circumstances, modifies or amends the budget based on a cost-effective proposal.

Results or Output

Training proposals, budget modifications

Supporting Knowledge

- Is aware of situations that call for a budget modification
- Understands the budget amendment process

Supporting Skills

- Establishes criteria for when to amend the budget
- Selects appropriate options for budget modification requests
- Develops justifications for requests to amend the budget
- Provides documentation as part of the amendment
- Assertively negotiates requests to cut the training budget and attempts to maintain budget resources when appropriate

Supporting Attitudes

- Is flexible and willing to modify the budget when unforeseen circumstances arise

Role: Training Manager

Basic Project Management Competency 17: Assesses the Need to Create a Project Team

When asked, the training manager assesses a need and identifies when a project team needs to be created.

Results or Output

Project plan, project team, project report

Supporting Knowledge

- Understands the fundamental elements of project management process
- Knows how to initiate a project
- Given a specific project, knows how to create a project team

Supporting Skills

- Uses an established process to develop a project plan
- Takes appropriate steps to create a project team

Supporting Attitudes

- Is willing to direct a project and create a project team

Role: Training Manager

Advanced Project Managing Competency 17: Assesses the Need to Create a Project Team

The training manager takes the initiative to assess a need and identifies when a project team needs to be created.

Results or Output

Project plan, project team

Supporting Knowledge

- Understands the fundamental elements of project management process
- Knows how to initiate a project
- Given a specific project, knows how to create a project team

Supporting Skills

- Uses an established process to develop a project plan
- Takes appropriate steps to create a project team
- Includes all stakeholders in the project team

Supporting Attitude

- Is willing to direct a project and create a project team

Role: Training Manager

Basic Project Management Competency 18: Uses Project Management Tools Appropriately

The training manager manages projects using appropriate resources; reports interim results to the project sponsor when asked.

Results or Output

Project plan changes, project reports

Supporting Knowledge

- Understands the need to monitor and protect resources during a project
- Is aware of the required format for interim project reporting

Supporting Skills

- Uses project management tools appropriately to create interim project reports
- Conserves resources so they are used appropriately during the project

Supporting Attitudes

- Values the limited resources and encourages conservation when appropriate
- Values collaboration

Role: Training Manager

Advanced **Advanced Project Management Competency 18: Uses Project Management Tools Appropriately**

The training manager manages projects using appropriate resources and periodically reports interim results to the project sponsor.

Results or Output

Project plan changes, project reports

Supporting Knowledge

- Understands the need to monitor and protect resources during a project
- Is aware of the need to provide timely information to the project sponsor
- Is aware of various formats for interim project reporting
- Negotiates project plan changes

Supporting Skills

- Uses project management tools appropriately to create interim project reports
- Conserves resources so they are used appropriately during the project
- Encourages collaboration on the project team

Supporting Attitudes

- Values the patronage of the project sponsor
- Values the limited resources and encourages conservation when appropriate
- Values collaboration

Role: Training Manager

Basic Project Management Competency 19: Ends Projects Appropriately

The training manager disbands the project team after a final report and terminates the project.

Results or Output

Final project report

Supporting Knowledge

- Is aware of critical content of a final report
- Understands the need to terminate a project

Supporting Skills

- Compiles a final project report
- Terminates the project

Supporting Attitude

- Is efficient

Role: Training Manager

Advanced ⚠️ *Advanced Competency 19: Ends Projects Appropriately*

The training manager disbands the project team after a final report and terminates the project.

Results or Output

Final project report

Supporting Knowledge

- Is aware of critical content of a final report
- Understands the need to terminate a project and disband a project team

Supporting Skills

- Compiles a final project report
- Passes organizational learning to other teams
- Terminates the project

Supporting Attitude

- Gives recognition to team members appropriately

Role: Training Manager

Basic Internal Consulting Competency 20: Acts as an Internal Consultant to the Client

Training manager's priorities are to act primarily as a department head and an advisor to course developers and trainers and to respond to requests from user departments.

Results or Output

Training department activity reports

Supporting Knowledge

- Understands how to use and support the course design process
- Understands how to support trainers
- Understands how to build relationships within the department

Supporting Skills

- Uses interpersonal skills to seek outcomes in the best interest of the department
- Uses a course design and training skills to give feedback and support within the department

Supporting Attitudes

- Values the development role

Role: Training Manager

Advanced Internal Consulting Competency 20: Acts as an Internal Consultant to the Client

Training manager's priorities are to act primarily as an internal consultant to the client, act as an advisor to course developers and trainers.

Results or Output

Consulting plan, a consulting process, department activity reports

Supporting Knowledge

- Understands how to use a consulting process
- Understands how to build a relationship with a client and within the department
- Understands how to use and support the course design process

Supporting Skills

- Identifies and confirms the actual client
- Uses interpersonal skills to seek outcomes in the best interest of the client
- Uses a systematic consulting process

Supporting Attitudes

- Values the supportive role
- Values the development role

Role: Training Manager

 Basic Internal Consulting Competency 21: Selects the Appropriate Role for Each Situation

The training manager usually selects the questioner, problem solver, trainer, and advisor roles when working with internal clients.

Results or Output

Agreed-on outcomes

Supporting Knowledge

- Understands the differences among two to three of the seven roles of an internal consultant and when to use each

Supporting Skills

- Assesses a situation to select the appropriate role

- Uses two to three of the internal consultant roles and sometimes transitions from one role to another

- Follows the role requested by the internal client

Supporting Attitude

- Is interested in success and in using familiar roles

Role: Training Manager

Advanced

Advanced Internal Consulting Competency 21: Selects the Appropriate Role for Each Situation

The internal consultant selects one of these roles, based on the requirements of the intervention: observer, facilitator, questioner, problem solver, trainer, advisor, or director.

Results or Output

Agreed-on outcomes

Supporting Knowledge

- Understands the differences among the seven roles of an internal consultant and when to use each

Supporting Skills

- Assesses a situation to select the appropriate role
- Uses a range of roles and smoothly transitions from one role to another
- Contracts with the client and sets boundaries for role clarity

Supporting Attitude

- Is willing to go beyond familiar or comfortable roles when required

Role: Training Manager

Basic Internal Consulting Competency 22: Uses a Systematic Internal Consulting Process

A systematic process contains some of these steps: (1) assesses the client contact to clarify who in the organization is requesting assistance and what they propose; (2) conducts needs assessment to develop relevant information; (3) recommends a training solution when appropriate; (4) conducts the training; and (5) evaluates the results.

Results or Output

Needs assessment data, training program

Supporting Knowledge

- Understands contents for needs assessments and the role of training
- Is aware of how to measure results

Supporting Skills

- Conducts needs assessments
- Designs training programs
- Conducts training
- Evaluates training for reaction and learning

Supporting Attitude

- Is willing to defer to internal client's request for training

Role: Training Manager

Advanced

Advanced Internal Consulting Competency 22: Uses a Systematic Internal Consulting Process

A systematic process contains these eight steps: (1) assesses the client contact to clarify who in the organization is requesting assistance and what they propose; (2) uses fact-finding to explore the scope of the project; (3) contracts for an outcome or result; (4) conducts needs assessment to develop relevant information; (5) develops a performance improvement plan; (6) conducts the intervention; (7) evaluates the results; and (8) integrates new learning.

Results or Output

Needs assessment data, training program, performance improvement plan, measurable results from an intervention

Supporting Knowledge

- Understands content for needs assessments and performance improvement plans
- Is aware of how to measure results

Supporting Skills

- Uses interpersonal skills to build a relationship with the client
- Conducts needs assessments
- Develops performance improvement plans
- Conducts interventions
- Evaluates interventions for results

Supporting Attitudes

- Is willing to follow the information and avoid a predetermined outcome
- Is willing to focus on results, not activities
- Shows determination to stay with a proven process
- Has the client's best interests as the internal consultant's priority

Training Manager Development Plan

Following the completion of a competency checklist, create a development plan that identifies the training manager's strengths, identifies areas for coaching and feedback, and identifies missing knowledge and skills, along with resources for development. Beginning a development plan with a training manager's strengths acknowledges that these strengths can be built on for further development. Strengths can also be used to mentor others. Areas for coaching and feedback can be competencies that were not observed. These may be competencies that require more practice because the training manager may already have supporting knowledge and attitudes, but did not display the skill. Areas can be deficient because some knowledge, skills, or attitudes are missing. Some of the areas may also be missing because the training manager's situation does not allow the use of these areas. Refer to the secondary checklists to identify what is missing and to plan what resources are available to build these competencies.

Gain agreement from management for the commitment of resources for development. Agree on a time frame for the development and re-evaluation of the competency.

A sample Training Manager Development Plan Template is on the next page.

Training Manager Development Plan Template

1. List competencies that exceed expectation:

2. Identify

Underdeveloped or unobserved competencies	Knowledge, skills, and attitudes to acquire

3. Identify competencies that require coaching and feedback:

4. Identify resources required to develop these competencies:

Target date for re-evaluation:

CHAPTER 7

Training Coordinator Competencies

Chapter Objectives

- To identify the competencies required of a training coordinator
- To learn how to use the competency checklists
- To create a training coordinator development plan

Chapter Tools

- Competency Model Checklist for Training Coordinators
- Expanded Competency Checklist for Training Coordinators
- Training Coordinator Development Plan Template

Assessment Questions

- What are the competencies for a training coordinator?
- How can these competencies be measured?
- What competencies apply to your role as a training coordinator?

Competencies Required of a Training Coordinator

Training coordinators are responsible for most of the administrative work in a training function. Planning, administrative, and liaison competencies are required for an effective training function.

A training coordinator's background is usually from one of three areas. First, a training coordinator can be an administrative assistant who is used to handling a variety of support functions and usually reports to a human resources manager. Second, a training coordinator can be a training professional who trains others and completes a variety of administrative tasks. Third, a training coordinator can be a manager or supervisor of a function or can be a department-of-one. Since the "department-of-one" calls for a unique combination of responsibilities, we discuss those competencies separately in Chapter 8.

A variety of titles for a training coordinator include some of these emerging titles: learning liaison officer, learning compliance specialist, training administrator, and training administrative assistant.

Competency Checklists for Training Coordinators

Following are two checklists that list and define planning, administrative, and liaison competencies for the training coordinator. When compiled they become a competency model for the training coordinator.

All the competencies together describe the optimum behaviors required. When reviewing competencies for a training coordinator, assess whether the training coordinator does the tasks described. Ratings of "A" and "B" distinguish whether the competency is held at the "advanced" or "basic" level. For either an "A" or "B" rating, tangible results or output are visible. A rating of "I" stands for "incomplete" because tangible results or output are not observed, are missing, or are partially complete. Remember that a competency is either observed or is not observed.

Following the Training Coordinator Competency Model Checklist is the second set of checklists. The first checklist expands on each of the numbered training coordinator competencies and provides a description of the *basic* competency along with supporting knowledge, skills, and attitudes. Results or output for each competency are also provided. Another checklist is provided with *advanced* competency descriptions with supporting knowledge, skills, and attitudes. At the end of the Competency Model Checklist the rater shows the total percentage of competencies observed. Remember to decide prior to the observation what percentage of competencies must be present to show competence. See Chapter 9 for information about using competencies as part of a certification process.

How to Use the Competency Checklists

To customize the training coordinator competency model, first review all the checklists. Next, select those competencies that are either required or desirable for the training coordinator role in your organization. Download the desired checklists from the CD that accompanies this book to create a customized checklist. Either eliminate the competencies that do not apply or rate the competency as N/A for "not applicable." Prior to assessing a competency, agree with the rater on the meaning of each competency. If the training coordinator is unsure whether to measure a basic or advanced competency, download both descriptions. If the checklists are not for a self-assessment, review the expanded descriptions with supporting knowledge, skills, and attitudes to ensure a shared definition of each competency and what level of competency is being assessed. See the resource section at the back of this book for sample completed assessments and development plans.

Competency Model Checklist for Training Coordinators

A = meets *advanced* competency (advanced tangible results or outputs are visible)

B = meets *basic* competency (tangible results or outputs are visible)

I = *incomplete* (tangible results or outputs are not observed, missing or partially complete)

N = behavior *not* observed (not competent)

Rating	Training Coordinator Competency	Basic Results or Output	Advanced Results or Output
	Planning Competencies		
	1. Identifies solutions to organizational problems	Written training plan	Actions to direct the training coordinator extracted from a written training plan
	2. Sets objectives for training events	Written objectives	Written objectives
	3. Helps line managers and supervisors identify training needs	Needs assessment data	Needs assessment data
	4. Develops resources	Resource database Reports	Resource database Reports Criteria for resource selection
	5. Buys packaged training programs	Library of training packages	Library of training packages
	6. Maintains corporate library	Books, periodicals, and other resources List of resources	Books, periodicals, and other resources List of resources
	7. Schedules training	Published schedule	Published schedule
	8. Evaluates the success of training efforts	Summary of participant evaluations, scored tests of participants, summarized skill development checklists, training cost information	Trend analysis of participant evaluations Completed tests of participants Completed skill development checklists Return on investment reports

Rating	Training Coordinator Competency	Basic Results or Output	Advanced Results or Output
	Administrative Competencies		
	9. Coordinates off-site facility arrangements	Facility contracts	Facility contracts
	10. Runs trainee registration and confirmation systems	Class rosters Confirmation letters Employee transcripts Charge-back notices Certificates of attendance Attendance reports	Database system templates Class rosters Confirmation letters Employee transcripts Charge-back notices Certificates of attendance Attendance reports
	11. Monitors tuition reimbursement programs	Reimbursement records	Reimbursement records Reimbursement reports
	12. Identifies training costs	Training cost list	Training budget
	13. Prepares training rooms for instruction	Room layout diagrams Set-up schedule Audiovisual and handout materials, name tents, evaluation forms	Room layout diagrams Set-up schedule Audiovisual and handout materials, name tents, evaluation forms
	14. Orders and inventories supplies	Purchase order log Inventory report	Purchase order log Inventory report
	15. Maintains audiovisual equipment	Equipment maintenance checklists Job aids to troubleshoot equipment Equipment check-out log	Equipment maintenance checklists Job aids to troubleshoot equipment Equipment check-out log
	Liaison Competencies		
	16. Hires external consultants	Requests for proposal Consultant contracts	Scope of work template Requests for proposal Consultant contracts
	17. Coaches subject-matter experts as trainers	Training problem referral	Training competency checklists
	18. Markets training internally	Marketing plan Training announcements	Marketing plan Training announcements
	% Total of competencies observed		
	% Total required for competence		

Expanded Competency Checklist for Training Coordinators

Role: Training Coordinator

Basic Planning Competency 1: Identifies Solutions to Organizational Problems

A training plan is written by others to provide direction for solutions to organizational problems that training can impact.

Results or Output

Actions to direct the training coordinator extracted from a written training plan

Supporting Knowledge

- Is aware of how training issues are extracted from organizational data

Supporting Skill

- Implements a training plan based on current organizational issues

Supporting Attitude

- Accurately follows the directions of others regarding the written training plan

---

Role: Training Coordinator

Advanced Planning Competency 1: Identifies Solutions to Organizational Problems

The training coordinator explores organizational problems and extracts and documents training issues. A training plan is written that provides solutions to the problems.

Results or Output

Written training plan

Supporting Knowledge

- Identifies organizational problems that contain training issues
- Is aware of funding sources

Supporting Skills

- Creates a training plan based on current organizational issues
- Develops relationships for funding sources

Supporting Attitudes

- Is open to developing relationships
- Deals fairly with resource suppliers

Role: Training Coordinator

B *Basic Planning Competency 2: Sets Objectives for Training Events*

Basic Reviews objectives for training events that are specific, measurable, attainable, realistic, and time-bound.

Results or Output

Written objectives

Supporting Knowledge

- Is aware of completely written objectives
- Is aware of the role objectives have in the success of training events

Supporting Skills

- Reviews training objectives
- Implements objectives with support of internal customers

Supporting Attitude

- Is willing to compromise or renegotiate when needed

Role: Training Coordinator

Advanced **Advanced Planning Competency 2: Sets Objectives for Training Events**

Set objectives for training events that are specific, measurable, attainable, realistic, and time-bound.

Results or Output

Written objectives

Supporting Knowledge

- Is aware of how to write useful objectives

Supporting Skills

- Writes training objectives
- Negotiates objectives with internal customers

Supporting Attitude

- Is willing to compromise or renegotiate when needed

Role: Training Coordinator

 Basic ***Basic Planning Competency 3: Helps Line Managers and Supervisors Identify Training Needs***

Gathers and summarizes needs assessment information developed by others.

Results or Output

Needs assessment data

Supporting Knowledge

- Is aware of sources for different types of needs assessments
- Understands how to compile and summarize needs assessment information using a variety of formats

Supporting Skills

- Summarizes needs assessment data
- Suggests tentative conclusions from raw data
- As part of a team, identifies training needs

Supporting Attitude

- Is willing to support decision makers with information

Role: Training Coordinator

 Advanced ***Advanced Planning Competency 3: Helps Line Managers and Supervisors Identify Training Needs***

Conducts needs assessments that include performance analysis, target population analysis, and task analysis.

Results or Output

Needs assessment data

Supporting Knowledge

- Is aware of types of needs assessments
- Understands which type of needs analysis produces specific types of data

Supporting Skills

- Conducts needs assessments
- Summarizes needs assessment data
- Suggests appropriate conclusions from raw data
- Identifies training needs
- Makes alternative recommendations for non-training needs

Supporting Attitude

- Is willing to allow the data to identify appropriate direction, rather than obtain data to support a predetermined conclusion

Role: Training Coordinator

Basic Planning Competency 4: Develops Resources

Maintains a list of suggested resources to include consultants, materials, and facilities for the training function.

Results or Output

Resource data base

Supporting Knowledge

- Is aware of how to classify different types of resources
- Understand database software

Supporting Skills

- Enters resources on a database
- Updates resource database on a regular basis
- Retrieves resource information in appropriately formatted reports

Supporting Attitude

- Is willing to give attention to detail

Role: Training Coordinator

Advanced ### *Advanced Planning Competency 4: Develops Resources*

Identifies a variety of resources to include consultants, materials, and facilities for the training function.

Results or Output

Resource database

Supporting Knowledge

- Is aware of resources
- Understands database software

Supporting Skills

- Solicits resources for inclusion in the database
- Distinguishes resources as appropriate from inappropriate
- Enters resources on a database
- Updates resource database on a regular basis
- Retrieves resource information in appropriately formatted reports

Supporting Attitude

- Is willing to give attention to detail

Role: Training Coordinator

Basic Planning Competency 5: Buys Packaged Training Programs

When directed, buys appropriate and effective training packages that meet a specific training need.

Results or Output

Library of training packages

Supporting Knowledge

- Is aware of resources for training packages
- Understands organization's procurement process

Supporting Skills

- Recommends ways to fill deficiencies in the organization's resources
- Complies with the requirements of the procurement process

Supporting Attitudes

- Is ethical and believes in fair treatment of vendors

Role: Training Coordinator

Advanced **Advanced Planning Competency 5: Buys Packaged Training Programs**

The training coordinator buys appropriate and effective training packages that meet specific training needs.

Results or Output

Library of training packages

Supporting Knowledge

- Is aware of resources for training packages
- Understands organization's procurement process

Supporting Skills

- Recommends ways to fill deficiencies in the organization's resources
- Selects training packages that are appropriate to the target audience and effectively meet the organization's learning needs
- Negotiates with vendors by explaining needs and asks for special consideration
- Complies with the requirements of the procurement process

Supporting Attitude

- Is ethical and believes in fair treatment of vendors

Role: Training Coordinator

Basic Planning Competency 6: Maintains Corporate Library

The training coordinator maintains and, when directed, adds items to a corporate library.

Results or Output

Books, periodicals, and other resources; list of resources

Supporting Knowledge

- Is aware of sources of library materials
- Understands the procurement process

Supporting Skills

- Recommends books, periodicals, and other resources that are appropriate and effectively meet the organization's learning needs
- Complies with the requirements of the procurement process
- Physically organizes resources so they can be located easily
- When directed, publicizes the corporate library holdings and the means to access library holdings
- Checks out materials, follows up on special requests, and retrieves non-returned materials

Supporting Attitudes

- Makes materials available to all employees
- Treats vendors fairly

Role: Training Coordinator

Advanced **Advanced Planning Competency 6: Maintains Corporate Library**
The training coordinator maintains and builds a corporate library.

Results or Output

Books, periodicals, and other resources; list of resources

Supporting Knowledge

- Is aware of sources of library materials
- Understands the procurement process

Supporting Skills

- Selects books, periodicals, and other resources that are appropriate and that effectively meet the organization's learning needs
- Complies with the requirements of the procurement process
- Physically organizes resources so they can be located easily
- Publicizes the corporate library holdings and means to access library holdings
- Checks out materials, follows up on special requests, and retrieves non-returned materials

Supporting Attitudes

- Makes materials available to all employees
- Treats vendors fairly

Role: Training Coordinator

Basic Planning Competency 7: Schedules Training

The training coordinator creates and gets approval for a training schedule that is compatible with business needs and cycles.

Results or Output

Published schedule

Supporting Knowledge

- Is aware of organization's holidays
- Understands database software
- Is aware of trainers' expertise and availability when asking trainers to teach classes
- Is aware of room configurations and capacity
- Is aware of the schedule approval process

Supporting Skills

- Uses database software to create a schedule
- Seeks approval for the training schedule
- Sets an optimum schedule of training classes
- Resolves scheduling conflicts

Supporting Attitude

- Is willing to negotiate with trainers, supervisors, and trainees to create an optimum schedule

Role: Training Coordinator

Advanced *Planning Competency 7: Schedules Training*

The training coordinator creates a training schedule that is compatible with business needs and cycles.

Results or Output

Published schedule

Supporting Knowledge

- Understands business needs and their impact on the training schedule
- Is aware of organization's holidays
- Understands database software
- Is aware of trainers' expertise when assigning trainers to teach classes
- Is aware of room configurations and capacity

Supporting Skills

- Uses database software to create a schedule
- Sets an optimum schedule of training classes
- Resolves scheduling conflicts
- Publicizes rescheduled classes and newly added classes

Supporting Attitude

- Is willing to negotiate with trainers, supervisors, and trainees to create an optimum schedule

Role: Training Coordinator

Basic Planning Competency 8: Evaluates the Success of Training Efforts

The training coordinator uses Donald Kirkpatrick's four levels of evaluation[1] to measure the success of training efforts as directed.

Results or Output

Summary of participant evaluations, scored tests of participants, summarized skill development checklists, training cost information

Supporting Knowledge

- Is aware of four levels of evaluation
- Understands how to summarize participant reaction sheet data
- Understands how to correct tests that measure learning
- Understands how to summarize skill performance checklist data
- Is aware of how to gather training costs

Supporting Skills

- Summarizes participant reaction sheets, in some cases using online software
- Corrects tests
- Summarizes skill performance checklist data
- Gathers training cost information

Supporting Attitude

- Is willing to summarize data correctly

[1]Kirkpatrick, Donald L. *Evaluating Training Programs: The Four Levels*. San Francisco: Berrett-Koehler, 1994.

Role: Training Coordinator

Advanced

Advanced Planning Competency 8: Evaluates the Success of Training Efforts

The training coordinator uses Donald Kirkpatrick's four levels of evaluation[2] to measure the success of training efforts.

Results or Output

Trend analysis of participant evaluations, completed tests of participants, completed skill development checklists, return on investment reports

Supporting Knowledge

- Understands four levels of evaluation and how each is measured
- Understands trend analysis created from participant reaction data
- Understands ways to measure learning
- Understands how to measure skill performance changes back on the job
- Understands return on investment measurement

Supporting Skills

- Summarizes participant reaction sheets, in some cases using online software
- Develops or customizes participant reaction sheets for each training event
- Develops trend analysis reports from participant reaction data
- Compiles statistics from instruments that measure learning
- Compiles statistics from skill performance data
- Creates a return-on-investment report as a feasibility analysis and post-training analysis
- Communicates evaluation information to management in a timely manner

Supporting Attitude

- Is willing to collect and analyze data objectively

---

[2]Kirkpatrick, Donald L. *Evaluating Training Programs: The Four Levels.* San Francisco: Berrett-Koehler, 1994.

Role: Training Coordinator

Basic Administrative Competency 9: Coordinates Off-Site Facility Arrangements

Given criteria, the training coordinator identifies appropriate off-site facilities for training events and negotiates with off-site facilities for the best value within budget guidelines.

Results or Output

Facility contracts

Supporting Knowledge

- Understands organization's needs and requirements to use an off-site facility
- Is aware of the organization's criteria for off-site meeting facilities
- Is aware of off-site resources to meet the organization's needs
- Understands different roles for off-site personnel

Supporting Skills

- Identifies appropriate off-site facilities that meet the organization's needs and requirements
- Negotiates with off-site facilities to get the best value within budget guidelines
- Troubleshoots problems that occur before, during, and after training events

Supporting Attitude

- Is willing to compromise during negotiations with off-site resources while remaining within budget guidelines

Role: Training Coordinator

Advanced

Advanced Administrative Competency 9: Coordinates Off-Site Facility Arrangements

The training coordinator identifies appropriate off-site facilities for training events and negotiates with off-site facilities for the best value.

Results or Output

Facility contracts

Supporting Knowledge

- Understands organization's needs and requirements to use an off-site facility

- Is aware of the organization's criteria for off-site meeting facilities

- Is aware of off-site resources to meet the organization's needs

- Understands different roles for off-site personnel

Supporting Skills

- Makes recommendations to set guidelines for off-site meeting facilities

- Identifies appropriate off-site facilities that meet the organization's needs and requirements

- Negotiates with off-site facilities to get the best value

- Builds a relationship with off-site facilities personnel for frequently used sites

- Periodically reviews contracts to assure the best value for facility use

- Troubleshoots problems that occur before, during, and after training events

Supporting Attitudes

- Is willing to compromise during negotiations with off-site resources when appropriate

- Is interested in seeking the best value to meet organization's needs for an off-site facility

Role: Training Coordinator

Basic Administrative Competency 10: Runs Trainee Registration and Confirmation Systems

The training coordinator operates software for a trainee registration and confirmation system.

Results or Output

Class rosters, confirmation letters, employee transcripts, charge-back notices, certificates of attendance, attendance reports

Supporting Knowledge

- Is aware of the capability of various systems currently used in the training function
- Is aware of how the system operates

Supporting Skills

- Enters accurate data into the system
- Produces class rosters
- Produces and sends confirmation letters to training participants and supervisors
- Produces complete and accurate employee transcripts
- Generates charge-back notices
- Produces certificates of attendance

Supporting Attitudes

- Pays attention to detail
- Assures the privacy of personnel records

Role: Training Coordinator

 Advanced

Advanced Administrative Competency 10: Runs Trainee Registration and Confirmation Systems

The training coordinator operates software for a trainee registration and confirmation system.

Results or Output

Class rosters, confirmation letters, employee transcripts, charge-back notices, certificates of attendance

Supporting Knowledge

- Is aware of the capability of various current and potential systems used in the training function
- Is aware of how the system operates

Supporting Skills

- Makes recommendations to purchase a database system based on criteria
- Creates templates for system output
- Enters accurate data into the system
- Produces class rosters
- Produces and sends confirmation letters to training participants
- Produces complete and accurate employee transcripts
- Generates charge-back notices
- Produces certificates of attendance

Supporting Attitudes

- Pays attention to detail
- Assures privacy of personnel records

Role: Training Coordinator

Basic Administrative Competency 11: Monitors Tuition Reimbursement Programs

The training coordinator compiles information, monitors, and maintains accurate records for tuition reimbursement program.

Results or Output

Reimbursement records

Supporting Knowledge

- Is aware of reimbursement requirements
- Understands how the database software operates

Supporting Skills

- Publicizes and updates tuition reimbursement information
- Ensures the accuracy of data input into the system
- Obtains management approval for reimbursement to employees of tuition expenditures

Supporting Attitude

- Maintains privacy of personnel records

Role: Training Coordinator

Advanced

Advanced Administrative Competency 11: Monitors Tuition Reimbursement Programs

The training coordinator compiles information, monitors, and maintains accurate records for tuition reimbursement program.

Results or Output

Reimbursement records

Supporting Knowledge

- Is aware of reimbursement requirements
- Understands how the database software operates

Supporting Skills

- Publicizes and updates tuition reimbursement information
- Ensures the accuracy of data input into the system
- Judges whether tuition reimbursement requirements are met
- Obtains management approval for reimbursement to employees of tuition expenditures
- Compiles reports as appropriate
- Complies with organization and legal requirements
- Manages the confidentiality of employee records

Supporting Attitude

- Maintains privacy of personnel records

Role: Training Coordinator

Basic Administrative Competency 12: Identifies Training Costs

The training coordinator tracks expenditures and reports on irregularities on a monthly or as-needed basis.

Results or Output

List of training costs

Supporting Knowledge

- Understands the importance of tracking training costs
- Is aware of techniques to report irregularities

Supporting Skills

- Tracks training expenditures
- Reports irregularities on a monthly or as-needed basis
- Corrects errors as directed

Supporting Attitude

- Values integrity and accuracy in budget oversight

Role: Training Coordinator

Advanced

Advanced Administrative Competency 12: Identifies Training Costs

The training coordinator tracks expenditures and reports on irregularities on a monthly or as-needed basis.

Results or Output

Budget reports

Supporting Knowledge

- Understands the importance of tracking a budget
- Is aware of techniques to monitor a budget

Supporting Skills

- Uses software to monitor a budget by tracking expenditures
- Reports irregularities on a monthly or as-needed basis
- Corrects errors

Supporting Attitude

- Values integrity and accuracy in budget oversight

Role: Training Coordinator

Basic Administrative Competency 13: Prepares Training Rooms for Instruction

The training coordinator physically sets up training rooms at the direction of the trainer and assures that all needed equipment and supplies are available.

Results or Output

Room layout diagrams, set-up schedule, audiovisual equipment and handout materials, name tents, evaluation forms

Supporting Knowledge

- Is aware of different types of room layouts
- Is aware of what equipment and supplies are required for different training events

Supporting Skills

- Duplicates and distributes pre-work for learning events
- Physically sets up room to trainer's requirements
- Assures equipment is working and in place
- Assures training supplies and materials are available in the training room
- Calls technicians to troubleshoot set-up needs

Supporting Attitudes

- Is flexible to make last-minute adjustments
- Is concerned to make the training event run smoothly

Role: Training Coordinator

Advanced Administrative Competency 13: Prepares Training Rooms for Instruction

The training coordinator physically sets up training rooms with optimum layout for the type of training to be presented and assures that all needed equipment and supplies are available. This competency includes setting up the virtual classroom for online learning events.

Results or Output

Room layout diagrams, set-up schedule, audiovisual equipment and handout materials, name tents, evaluation forms

Supporting Knowledge

- Understands how room layout affects learning dynamics
- Is aware of what equipment and supplies are required for different training events

Supporting Skills

- Duplicates and distributes pre-work for learning events
- Physically sets up room to trainer's requirements
- Assures equipment is working and in place
- Assures training supplies and materials are available in the training room
- Troubleshoots set-up needs

Supporting Attitudes

- Is flexible to make last-minute adjustments
- Is concerned to make the training event run smoothly

Role: Training Coordinator

Basic Administrative Competency 14: Orders and Inventories Supplies

The training coordinator monitors an inventory of training supplies and orders supplies when directed.

Results or Output

Purchase order log, inventory report

Supporting Knowledge

- Is aware of where supplies are located
- Understands the inventory process
- Understands the purchasing process

Supporting Skills

- Takes an accurate inventory on a monthly basis or as needed
- Generates an inventory report
- Orders supplies when directed using the purchase order system
- Receives ordered supplies and matches the purchase order to the packing list
- Stocks supplies in an orderly manner
- Sends invoices for received supplies to management

Supporting Attitudes

- Conserves organization resources to thwart theft of supplies
- Treats vendors fairly

Role: Training Coordinator

Advanced Administrative Competency 14: Orders and Inventories Supplies

The training coordinator monitors inventory of training supplies and orders supplies when directed or when the inventory goes below par. Par is the established number of a specific item needed on hand at any time.

Results or Output

Purchase order log, inventory report

Supporting Knowledge

- Is aware of where supplies are located and the par for each item
- Understands the purchasing process

Supporting Skills

- Takes an accurate inventory on a monthly basis or as needed
- Generates an inventory report
- Orders supplies when needed using the purchase order system
- Receives ordered supplies and matches the purchase order to the packing list
- Stocks supplies in an orderly manner
- Approves invoices for received supplies and forwards them to accounts payable
- Reviews supply list regularly to update needs and remove obsolete items as needed

Supporting Attitudes

- Conserves organizational resources to thwart theft of supplies
- Treats vendors fairly

Role: Training Coordinator

Basic Administrative Competency 15: Maintains Audiovisual Equipment

The training coordinator initiates repair requests when asked and maintains a preventive maintenance schedule for each piece of equipment.

Results or Output

Equipment maintenance checklists, job aid to troubleshoot equipment, equipment check-out log

Supporting Knowledge

- Is aware of preventive maintenance schedules
- Is aware of resources to maintain equipment

Supporting Skills

- Requests preventive maintenance for equipment
- Calls approved vendors for maintenance when directed
- Recommends payment approval for maintenance invoices
- Adds new equipment to the maintenance checklist

Supporting Attitudes

- Conserves equipment and guards against theft
- Treats service vendors fairly

Role: Training Coordinator

Advanced Administrative Competency 15: Maintains Audiovisual Equipment

The training coordinator keeps audiovisual equipment in working order and maintains a preventive maintenance schedule for each piece of equipment.

Results or Output

Equipment maintenance checklists, job aid to troubleshoot equipment, equipment check-out log

Supporting Knowledge

- Is aware of preventive maintenance schedules
- Is aware of resources to maintain equipment

Supporting Skills

- Requests preventive maintenance for equipment
- Selects appropriate resources for maintenance
- Approves maintenance or services invoices for payment
- Adds new equipment to the maintenance checklist
- Troubleshoots minor repairs

Supporting Attitudes

- Conserves organizational resources to thwart theft of supplies
- Treats vendors fairly

Role: Training Coordinator

 Basic Liaison Competency 16: Hires External Consultants

When a need is identified for which internal resources are not available, the training coordinator recommends an external vendor using the appropriate process.

Results or Output

Requests for proposal, consultant contracts, agreements, or memoranda of understanding

Supporting Knowledge

- Is aware of the appropriate process to hire an external consultant
- Is aware of elements of a request for proposal
- Is aware of elements of consultant contracts, agreements, or memoranda of understanding

Supporting Skills

- Creates a request for proposal from a scope-of-work template for the desired external resources
- Uses an objective process to evaluate consultant proposals
- Recommends hiring of consultants who meet requirements and seeks budget approval of costs
- Monitors the contract and makes amendments as needed
- Recommends approval of consultant invoices

Supporting Attitude

- Treats external consultants fairly

Role: Training Coordinator

Advanced ### Advanced Liaison Competency 16: Hires External Consultants

When a need is identified for which internal resources are not available, the training coordinator selects an external vendor using the appropriate process.

Results or Output

Scope of work template, requests for proposal, consultant contracts, agreements, or memoranda of understanding

Supporting Knowledge

- Is aware of the appropriate process to hire an external consultant
- Understands elements of a request for proposal
- Understands elements of consultant contracts, agreements, or memoranda of understanding

Supporting Skills

- Creates a scope-of-work template
- Creates a request for proposal that contains an accurate scope of work for the desired external resources
- Uses an objective process to evaluate consultant proposals
- Negotiates contract elements with external consultants
- Recommends hiring of consultants who meet requirements and seeks budget approval of costs
- Monitors the contract and makes amendments as needed
- Approves consultant invoices

Supporting Attitudes

- Is interested in getting the best value for the organization
- Treats vendors fairly

Role: Training Coordinator

Basic Liaison Competency 17: Coaches Subject-Matter Experts as Trainers

Refers problems with subject-matter experts (SMEs) with training responsibilities to management. Supports SMEs' program design needs, materials development, and room arrangements.

Results or Output

Training problem referral

Supporting Knowledge

- Is aware of how to report training deficiencies
- Is aware of criteria to select SMEs as trainers

Supporting Skills

- Posts recruitment notices for SMEs as trainers
- Refers problems with subject-matter experts to management

Supporting Attitude

- Is willing to report problems

Role: Training Coordinator

Advanced Liaison Competency 17: Coaches Subject-Matter Experts as Trainers

The training coordinator selects, develops, and coaches subject-matter experts (SMEs) with training responsibilities. Supports SMEs' program design needs, materials development, and room arrangements. (Trainer competency checklists in Chapter 3 can be used to coach SMEs.)

Results or Output

Trainer competency checklists

Supporting Knowledge

- Understands adult learning principles
- Is aware of how to use trainer competency checklists
- Understands criteria to select SMEs as trainers

Supporting Skills

- Recruits SMEs as trainers
- Applies criteria to select SMEs as trainers
- Uses trainer competency checklists to coach and develop SMEs as trainers

Supporting Attitudes

- Applies the selection and development process fairly
- Is willing to coach SMEs to achieve desired results

Role: Training Coordinator

Basic Liaison Competency 18: Markets Training Internally

The training coordinator implements the marketing plan so that the target population is aware of training offerings.

Results or Output

Marketing plan, training announcements

Supporting Knowledge

- Understands marketing plan
- Is aware of elements of effective training announcements

Supporting Skills

- Creates attractive and effective training announcements
- Distributes training announcements using a variety of distribution channels on an effective timeline

Supporting Attitude

- Is efficient

Role: Training Coordinator

Advanced

Advanced Liaison Competency 18: Markets Training Internally

The training coordinator develops and uses all elements of a marketing strategy to assure the correct target population attends the right training events to build skills that will meet organizational needs.

Results or Output

Marketing plan, training announcements

Supporting Knowledge

- Understands marketing strategies
- Is aware of elements of effective training announcements
- Understands the difference between selling and marketing
- Understands the differences between marketing, publicity, and advertising

Supporting Skills

- Uses a variety of techniques to conduct an ongoing marketing effort
- Attends management and staff meetings to identify needs as part of market research
- Develops a collaborative marketing strategy for the training function
- Creates attractive and effective training announcements
- Distributes training announcements using an effective timeline
- Monitors the effectiveness of the marketing effort based on attendance

Supporting Attitude

- Is interested in matching employee needs with appropriate training solutions

Training Coordinator Development Plan

Following the completion of a competency checklist, create a development plan that identifies the training coordinator's strengths, identifies areas for coaching and feedback, and identifies missing knowledge and skills along with resources for development. Beginning a development plan with a training coordinator's strengths acknowledges what can be built on for further development. Strengths can also be used to mentor others. Areas for coaching and feedback can be competencies that were not observed. They may be competencies that require more practice because the training coordinator may already have supporting knowledge and attitudes, but does not display the skill. Some knowledge, skills, or attitudes may be missing. Refer to the secondary checklists to identify what is missing and to plan what resources are available to build these competencies.

Gain agreement from management for the commitment of resources for development. Agree on a time frame for the development and re-evaluation of the competency.

A sample Training Coordinator Development Plan Template is on the next page.

Training Coordinator Development Plan Template

Training Coordinator's Name: _____ Date: _____

1. List competencies that exceed expectation:

2. Identify

Underdeveloped or unobserved competencies	Knowledge, skills, and attitudes to acquire

3. Identify competencies that require coaching and feedback:

4. Identify resources required to develop these competencies:

Target date for re-evaluation:

CHAPTER 8

Being a Department of One

Chapter Objectives

- To learn to sort priorities
- To make a training plan

Chapter Tools

- Planning Checklist for a Department of One

Assessment Questions

- How are competing priorities assessed?
- What are the elements of an effective training plan?

Sorting Priorities

Training professionals who find they are the entire training function face unique challenges and several choices. Organizations sometimes have unrealistic expectations of what a department-of-one trainer can accomplish. To meet the challenge of constantly being in a reactive or crisis mode, begin by asking several strategic questions and taking several planning actions.

First, find out why this particular training function exists. This will help establish a business focus for the function and help define its mission. Next, review the advantages and disadvantages of where the training function reports. (These points were identified in Chapter 1.) Create a plan to take advantage of where the function reports and identify how to overcome the disadvantages of where it reports.

Conduct a needs assessment by interviewing the organization's top managers. Based on the results of the assessment, develop a training plan. (How to develop a training plan is discussed in Chapter 5.) Finally, review the roles and competencies of the trainer or instructor, facilitator and coach, course designer, training manager, and training coordinator in Chapters 3 through 7. Identify the competencies that are needed to staff the department of one. Identify the strengths you have on which to build the training function and which competencies you need to develop. Identify internal and external resources that can help you meet the training needs and determine the budget available to meet those training needs.

Information derived from a needs assessment can help you sort priorities and bring clarity to a challenging and confusing situation. When you, as a department of one, begin to sort priorities and take an active and planned approach to the training function, you begin to build credibility, reduce stress, and experience success.

Competency Checklist for a Department of One

A Planing checklist for a department of one begins on the next page.

Planning Checklist for a Department of One

Use this planning checklist when starting a training function or joining an organization as a training department of one.

1. Why does the training function exist?

2. What are the business needs that are to be met by this function?

3. Where does training report in the organization?

4. What are the advantages and disadvantages of this reporting relationship?

5. How will you capitalize on the advantages and mitigate the disadvantages?

6. Identify training needs by conducting a needs assessment and interviewing top managers.

7. Develop a written training plan based on the needs assessment.

8. Meet with decision makers and present the training plan.

9. Review the training function roles and identify competencies needed by the person who staffs the department of one.

10. Identify internal resources available to meet the training needs.

11. Identify external resources needed to meet the training needs.

12. Determine how the budgetary approval process works.

Making a Training Plan

A training plan can be written for the short term (one quarter or one year) or a long-term period of time (more than one year). A training plan can also be written to meet a specific performance improvement need for a group of employees (for example, bank tellers take on an expanded role to be cross-trained in new accounts representative duties) or for an anticipated organizational need (rollout of a new product). There are ten parts to an effective and complete training plan, described below.

1. Define the Issues

Define the business issues that the plan needs to address. For example, if any of the following issues emerged in an organization, it would be appropriate to develop a training plan to address it.

- How can we reduce the talk time per call for Help Desk analysts while maintaining customer satisfaction at the same level?

- How can we eliminate the complaints from the public about the lack of professionalism among the office staff (how they appear and how they treat the public) in order for the city council person to fulfill the mission of the office?

- How can information systems analysts work in a more systematic fashion to solve user complaints efficiently and correctly?

- How can we train all salespeople to sell the features and benefits of the next version of our software products?

2. Reaffirm the Outcome, Results, or Objectives of the Plan

Determine why satisfying this business issue needs to be a priority. Describe what results would be shown with a successful outcome of the plan. If the plan objectives were achieved, what results would be shown? When the objectives, results, or outcomes are stated in measurable terms, part 6 of the plan is easier to develop. Identify obstacles that will have to be overcome for this result to be reached.

3. Clearly State the Performance Deficiency and Its Causes

Performance deficiencies must be stated in behavioral terms. Identify what the current target population *is currently doing,* and also state what the target population *should or ought to be doing.* What expectations are not being met by the target population? Stating the causes of the deficiency will also help justify the type of intervention described in step 8 below.

4. Establish Performance Standards

It is difficult to improve performance through training if no performance standards exist. Often training is requested by supervisors or managers to impart knowledge or skill as a means to improve performance—in short, to "fix it." Is there a performance standard to use as the goal for a minimum level of acceptable performance? The operational area can best establish job performance standards. The trainer or internal consultant can assist the operational area managers in developing job performance standards by conducting benchmarking interviews of "star" performers, customers, managers, and others.

5. Identify the Target Population

Who is to be included in the training plan? What job classifications do they hold? Are there secondary target populations that could also benefit from the training? How many people are involved? How will their supervisors and/or customers be involved? Can different levels of employees attend the same session? This information is critical to obtain prior to scheduling and for measuring the results and costs later.

6. Establish Evaluation Criteria

How will you know whether or not the training intervention is successful? How will the intervention be evaluated? How will the target population's reaction to the training be measured? How will learning be measured? How will the transfer of what was learned to the job be measured? How will bottom-line results be measured? The tools to measure the training are not developed at this point. Only a decision about how the training will be measured is made so far.

7. Describe the Proposed Intervention

This part of the training plan includes all activities to help the target population reach its objectives. Develop a rationale for each activity and the reasons for the sequence of the activities. This part of a training plan can include the following type of activities:

- Establish or clarify a policy
- Set up a process or procedure
- Create a job aid
- Distribute information (written or briefing presentation)
- Conduct a demonstration
- Conduct a training program
- Create individual action plans

Notice that even though this process is called creating a "training" plan, additional interventions besides training can be appropriate at this point. You will want to identify how to address any obstacles to each type of activity during the intervention.

8. Estimate the Cost of the Plan

What are the costs to carry out all phases of the plan? What is the cost of doing nothing? What is the feasibility of implementing this training plan? Over what period of time will the cost of the plan be recouped or expensed? It is essential to determine these costs prior to implementing the plan to establish a benchmark to later measure the plan's results.

9. Build a Partnership with Management

How will supervisors or managers of those involved in the intervention be included in the planning and follow-up for improved performance? Be sure to include supervisors and managers in the needs assessment process and to seek appropriate approvals and signatures as your plan development progresses.

10. Schedule

What time of the day, week, month, quarter, or year is best for the actions described in part 7 of the plan? What is the appropriate sequence of events described in part 7 of the plan?

Presenting a Training Plan

After writing a training plan, ask for feedback from a colleague who can give you insights into the strengths and weaknesses of your plan. When presenting a written training plan to management, provide an executive overview of the plan that takes no more than a page or two to cover all ten points. Begin by stating the purpose of the plan, why recommended actions are a priority, and how and from whom information was gathered. The main body of the plan should contain the detailed information on each part, how the information was developed, and a justification for any recommendation. Identify any obstacles and how they can be addressed.

Depending on the culture of your organization and how decisions are made, consider presenting the training plan in a live meeting. This allows the recipients of the plan the opportunity to ask questions that might arise. Most training plans are complex and have more than one or two recommendations. Your plan may have to be studied and considered before a decision is made. Don't expect an immediate decision in favor of the plan. Each organization has its own methods and timing for making decisions.

CHAPTER 9

How to Develop Internal Certification Programs

Chapter Objectives

- To list the reasons to develop a certification program in your organization
- To distinguish the benefits between internal and external certifying authorities
- To identify the difference between certificates and certification
- To learn how to use developed competencies to plan a certification program
- To learn how to demonstrate competence and understanding versus performing
- To plan how to introduce training competencies in the organization
- To learn how to use competencies for self, peer, and supervisory assessments
- To develop feedback and development processes

- To gain agreement on a certification program
- To identify cautions about using certification programs

Chapter Tools

- Checklist for Developing a Certification Program

Assessment Questions

- Why would my organization want to develop a certificate or certification program?
- What role do competencies play in developing a certification program?
- Who needs to be involved in developing a certification program?
- How can a certification program be introduced successfully in an organization?
- What are some problems and solutions that concern certification programs?

Developing a Certification Program in Your Organization

Certification is the process of demonstrating competence. Certification is often sought to gain prestige, promotion, attract customers, or meet a government requirement. Some organizations want to develop certification programs because they face some level of governmental regulation. Certification through training may be required to demonstrate compliance with those governmental regulations. Other organizations use certification programs as a marketing tool to advertise a level of competence to customers that a competitor might not have. Certification can help both manufacturing and service organizations promote superior products and services. Some manufacturers extend training and certification to customers who use their products, which promotes brand loyalty and may decrease help desk calls.

Consider conducting "guaranteed" training, promising that learners will take away new knowledge and skills that are used on the job. When guaranteeing training, the training function must start with well-designed training programs and certified instructors who can deliver on the guarantee.

Certification programs can promote employee loyalty, improve morale, and demonstrate to employees that the organization has an interest in developing and retaining them. Organizations must decide whether additional compensation can be earned by employees who earn certification.

Choosing Between Internal or External Certifying Authority

An organization must decide whether to establish its own certification program or use an outside certifying authority. Who is a certifying authority? Some colleges and universities conduct certification programs in general areas of study. For example, elementary and secondary teachers attend a course of study that includes student teaching or an intern program. The certifying authority for a teaching credential is the state in which the teacher wants to work.

In the area of training certification, external certifying authorities currently include some colleges and universities, trade associations, and private training and development vendors such as The Training Clinic, Friesen, Kaye and Associates, and Langevin Learning Services.

Often vendors who license their training programs to organizations require a certification process for internal trainers who will present their programs.

American trade associations who publish competencies and/or offer certification include The International Board of Standards for Training and Performance (IBSTPI), The Computing Technology Industry Association (CompTia), and the American Society for Training and Development (ASTD).

IBSTPI has developed competencies for instructors (1993 and 2003), course designers (2000), and training managers (1989, 2001). IBSTPI does not have a certification process. The Computing Technology Industry Association (CompTia) is an external certifying authority for technical trainers and offers a Certified Technical Trainer designation (CTT+) that is based on IBSTIP's instructor competencies. It does not offer course work to complete these competencies. Vendors can submit their courses for approval from CompTia. ASTD has conducted six studies of training models and competencies since 1978. ASTD is not a certifying authority at this time.

So why would an organization want to create its own certification program instead of using an outside certifying authority? First, the only external certifying authority from a professional association is CompTia, and their certification is limited to instructors. Although other trade associations provide competency studies for trainers, course designers, and training managers, The Training Clinic is the only organization to address competencies for training coordinators.

Second, until this book, no organization has offered competencies that can be used easily to establish a certification program. This book offers tools any organization can customize to fit its needs.

An organization can customize the competencies that are appropriate to its business, rather than use an entire model designed for all training professionals.

Defining Certificates and Certification

Most participants earn a *certificate* of attendance by attending all or most of a training program. The assumption behind a certificate of attendance is that participants who complete class activities meet the learning objectives and develop new knowledge and skills. However, certificates of attendance do not attest to learner competency if no test is given to demonstrate competency.

Certification implies that the learner passed a valid test and demonstrated competence. For example, The Training Clinic offers several certificates, but only one certification for a Certified Technical Training Specialist (CTTS) designation. This certification requires five days of course work, which is followed by a written test that includes both objective and essay questions. Participants then submit a videotaped lesson they have taught that demonstrates they have applied the skills learned and practiced during the workshop successfully. Participants must pass the written and videotaped lesson with a score of 75 percent or better to earn certification.

Another type of certification is used by Microsoft to have its trainers earn a designation of a Microsoft Certified Trainer (MCT). For certification, Microsoft requires attendance at a combination of approved technical courses and an approved train-the-trainer course. Vendors can receive approval for their courses by submitting their curriculum to an outside reviewing organization, which analyzes all course materials and matches them to competencies. Microsoft-approved train-the-trainer courses are mapped to the fourteen instructor competencies published by the International Board of Standards for Training (IBSTPI). Microsoft also has an annual recertification process that requires MCTs to attend a specific number of approved courses each year.

Thus, the difference between a certificate and certification is that most certificates require attendance; and most certifications require demonstration of new knowledge and skills. For purposes of demonstrating competencies, be sure to specify which your program provides.

Using Developed Competencies to Plan a Certificate or Certification Program

Begin by identifying the benefits sought through a certificate or certification program. Decide whether your organization will offer a certificate program (without testing) or a certification program (required testing). Decide which jobs or roles the organization will certify. While only five roles (training manager, training coordinator, course designer, trainer or instructor, facilitator or coach) were identified in earlier chapters of this book, the job or role could be a combination of responsibilities from more than one role. Analyze the role(s) and select the competencies that accurately reflect the role as carried out in your organization. This analysis and selection of competencies should involve all the stakeholders in the certification process. The CD that accompanies this book contains checklists that can be customized for selected roles.

The competency checklists show four ratings for the person being rated.

A = meets *advanced* competency (advanced tangible results or outputs are visible)

B = meets *basic* competency (tangible results or outputs are visible)

I = *incomplete* (tangible results or outputs are not observed, are missing, or partially complete)

N = behavior *not* observed (not competent)

The top two ratings show different levels of competence and that the behavior is present and that results and output are visible. Decide whether certification will be earned if an individual exhibits all, most, or a pre-determined percentage of the competencies. Decide how many opportunities someone has to raise a rating of "I" or "N" to A or B.

Decide over what period of time competencies will be observed to earn certification. It is likely that more than one or two observations will be needed to rate all the competencies chosen for a specific role.

Decide what rating is needed to earn certification. For example, if you select twenty-two trainer competencies and seek *advanced* certification, how many competencies must be rated at the *advanced* level to earn certification? For example, The Training Clinic requires a 75 percent positive observation to earn its CTTS designation.

Decide whether recertification is part of your organization's process. Once certification is earned, does the training manager, training coordinator, trainer or instructor, facilitator or coach, or course designer need to complete the certification process every year, every five years, or randomly depending on the organization's needs?

Demonstrating Competence and Understanding Versus Performing

How will employees in the training function demonstrate their competence? Perhaps the most effective method is to rate performance based on both knowledge and attitudes. While knowledge tests can verify WHAT a person understands, his or her competence is best demonstrated by a structured observation using a competency checklist. The competencies described in this book are based on observable behaviors, and the secondary checklists are based on showing one's underlying knowledge and attitudes.

To describe knowledge that supports a competency, the checklist uses verbs like "understands" or "is aware of." To rate the trainer's knowledge accurately, the rater and the trainer agree prior to the rating how both understanding and awareness will be demonstrated. Also, to describe attitudes that support a competency, the checklist uses verbs like "is sensitive" or "is concerned." To rate the trainer's attitude accurately, the rater and the trainer agree prior to the rating how these attitudes will be demonstrated.

Decide whether or not you will allow those who work in the training function to achieve certification through testing and observation without completing course work. If certification is based on demonstrating results and output, then it makes sense to allow candidates to demonstrate competence without attending classes. This is especially true if an experienced employee is hired into the training function.

Introducing Training Competencies in the Organization

Introducing competencies assumes that the highest level of management has approved the concept and practice of rating competencies and offering certification. Most of the organization's trainers would be involved in the process of developing competencies. If a collective bargaining unit represents trainers in your organization, it would be appropriate to involve that representative early in the planning and development process.

Competency and certification programs may have fuller participation and acceptance when the programs are voluntary, rather than mandated. After most or all of those in the training function become certified, it is easier to make certification a requirement for new employees entering the function.

Train those who will be candidates or observers in the process on how to use the competency checklists. Written descriptions of the competencies and certification process should be available to certification candidates. Having a single source of information on the process posted on an internal website will keep the process current. A knowledgeable person in the training function should be available to discuss the process with candidates and answer questions as they come up.

Decide whether monetary rewards will be a part of the certification process. If a certified trainer is considered to be a valued part of the training function, should that designation carry a salary increase or higher seniority with it? Be sure to discuss this decision with compensation experts in your organization.

Measuring Competencies: Self, Peer, and Supervisory Assessments

For a certification program to be seen as valid, there has to be a close correlation between the tasks performed as part of one's roles and responsibilities and the competencies measured. Seek agreement of various stakeholders and experts and have them match the tasks to the competencies that will become part of the certification program.

Decide who will observe and verify that competencies are present. The measurements will have greater meaning and be accepted more readily if three or more observers verify the presence of a competency. Start by asking the trainers or instructors to do a self-measurement of the selected competencies. Surprisingly, it is not unusual for those with fewer than five years' experience to rate themselves higher than those who have been in the function longer than five years rate themselves. Newer trainers are sometimes unconsciously incompetent. They don't know what they don't know, and it is sometimes difficult to convince them there is a lot of room for improvement.

In order to gain a realistic measurement of a trainer's competency, have at least two other knowledgeable observers complete a competency checklist about the person. Be sure the observers are trained in the use of the checklists and share the same definitions of terms. After agreeing on what supporting knowledge, skills, and attitudes need to be present, they should agree on what each competency looks like in practice, as well as how exceptional behaviors are demonstrated. When peers and supervisors are called on to rate trainers' competencies, it is most appropriate if they are experienced in the certification being sought. Decide what weight the self-evaluation, peer evaluation, and supervisor evaluation will have when measuring a competency. For example, supervisors' ratings may be given more credence. Some trainers also may ask their learners to assess their competencies.

As stated previously, decide on the percent of competencies required to earn certification. Be sure to publish all the policies regarding certification prior to beginning the certification process.

Setting Up Feedback and Development Processes

After someone in the training function has completed the measurement part of the certification process, decide what happens next. What if someone fails to exhibit a required competency or does not reach the required percent of competencies? Can the candidate repeatedly attempt certification? If so, how many times should a candidate attempt certification before it is suggested that he or she try another line of work? If some of the competencies are partially present or not observed, a development plan must become the basis for a feedback and coaching session. (Development Plan Templates are at the end of Chapters 3, 4, 5, 6, and 7, and on the CD accompanying this book.)

An organization that agrees to have a competency and certification process also has to commit to providing the resources to administer the process and to develop those who want to commit to a development plan. Resources can be internal or external, formal or informal, structured or unstructured. Providing training as a resource for development is an example of a formal and a structured resource. Job shadowing or informational interviewing are less formal and less structured developmental resources.

Time is perhaps the greatest resource. Decide how much time is appropriate for someone who wishes to complete a development plan and when another assessment of the person is appropriate.

Gaining Agreement on a Certification Program

If a certification program is to succeed, all stakeholders in the process must be involved at each step of the planning, development, and execution process. Requiring participation of all parties in each step is a good tool to gain their involvement and agreement. Agreement by consensus on each step in the process is desirable, but may be impractical. At the least, a majority agreement can keep the process from collapsing.

Using Certification Programs: Cautions

Certificate and certification programs with specific, limited purposes have the greatest opportunity of being fair, valued, and successful. Use great care when certification is tied to employment screening decisions, promotions, and terminations to avoid unfair or wrong decisions that could encourage a trainer to seek a legal remedy.

Any certification program must be validated through job/task analysis. When doing this type of analysis, include observation of typical performers who demonstrate the knowledge, skills, and attitudes. Be sure observations of typical performers are taken and measured under *typical* job conditions. While observing experts to validate a certification process is useful, experts are rarely typical performers.

The success of any certification program depends on the quality of the training program. Any organization offering certification must offer guaranteed training, that is, training that can be shown to impart knowledge and demonstrate skill transfer.

Checklist for Developing a Certification Program

Use this checklist as a summary of steps to establish a certificate/certification program.

_____Gain management buy-in for the certification program.

_____Decide which stakeholders will be included in setting up a certification program.

_____Decide whether you will offer a certificate or certification program.

_____Decide whether the certification process is voluntary or compulsory.

_____Agree on who will select the competencies for a specific certification program.

_____Validate the selected competencies and match them to job tasks.

_____Identify over what period of time certification can be sought.

_____Decide what percent of competencies are needed for certification.

_____Select the roles that will be certified.

_____Decide who will create and grade a test that demonstrates competency.

_____Select those who will observe and rate competencies (candidate, peer, supervisor, learners, customers).

_____Describe what behaviors will demonstrate knowledge and attitudes that support a competency.

_____Train those who will observe and rate competencies.

_____Decide whether certification can be achieved without completing course work.

_____Prepare certification candidates for the certification process.

_____Decide length of time allowed for course work to be completed.

_____Decide how often someone can attempt to raise a rating from "I" or "N" by re-testing or another observation.

_____Select monetary or other rewards that are tied to certification.

_____Identify who will complete the development plan (candidate, observer, both?).

_____Identify resources available to help the candidate complete the development plan.

_____Decide whether certification will be related to employment selection, promotion, transfer, or termination.

_____Publish the policies and procedures for the certification process.

RESOURCES

Sample Competency Checklists and Development Plans

Glossary

Bibiliography

Index

Sample Competency Checklists and Development Plans

The first sample is a self-assessment completed by a training manager with training responsibilities. She has ten years of experience in a training position and only presents technical training topics in classroom or on-the-job training sessions.

Sample 1: Competency Model Checklists for Trainers or Instructors

A = meets *advanced* competency (advanced tangible results or outputs are visible)

B = meets *basic* competency (tangible results or outputs are visible)

I = *incomplete* (tangible results or outputs are not observed, missing or partially complete)

N = behavior *not* observed (not competent)

Rating	Trainer or Instructor Competency	Basic Results or Output	Advanced Results or Output
B	1. Prepares for instruction	Training course announcement Pre-work assignments Room set-up diagram Training equipment materials	Management partnership Training course announcement Pre-work assignments Room set-up diagram Training equipment materials
B	2. Sets a learning environment	Active participants, completed introductions, posted participant learning objectives	Active participants, completed introductions, music, course graphic, name tents, materials, ground rules are set, objectives posted
A	3. Uses adult learning principles	Active participants	Active participants, different training methods to appeal to different learning styles
A	4. Uses lecture	Lecture notes, handout materials, visuals	Large group participation, answers participant questions, models platform techniques
B	5. Conducts discussions	Agenda, questions, summary of ideas	Agenda, questions, summary of ideas, group participation

Rating	Trainer or Instructor Competency	Basic Results or Output	Advanced Results or Output
I	6. Facilitates exercises	Participants complete exercises	Participants complete advanced exercises, such as case studies, games, and simulations
B	7. Conducts demonstrations	Completed product or completed process	Completed product or completed process, skill performance checklist
N	8. Uses role play	Role-play observer's critique sheet, skill development	Role-play observer's critique sheet, empathy or skill development
A	9. Gives feedback to learners	Negative feedback, learner changes behavior, and learner improves	Positive and negative feedback, learner changes behavior, and learner improves
B	10. Uses audiovisuals identical to handout materials	Equipment and media support handout materials	Equipment and media that
N	11. Administers tests and evaluates skill performance	Scored tests and completed skill performance checklists	Scored tests and completed skill performance checklists, timely feedback of test results
A	12. Handles problem learners from training	Problem ignored or problem learner excluded	Changed learner behavior
B	13. Manages appropriate use of technology	Use of technology	Use of technology
B	14. Promotes learning transfer	Transferred learning is used on the job	Transferred learning is used on the job
N	15. Conducts learning online	Completed lessons	Completed lessons
B	16. Recommends course modifications	Written requests for changes	Written recommendations for changes
75%	**Total of competencies observed**		
75%	**Total required for competence**		

(50 percent of the competencies are recorded at a "basic" level. 25 percent of the competencies are recorded at an "advanced" level. Added together, this trainer has achieved basic competency with a 75 percent score.)

Sample Trainer or Instructor Development Plan

Trainer's Name: _____Trainer A_____ Date: _____

1. List competencies that exceed expectation:

> 3. *Using adult learning principles*
>
> 4. *Uses lecture*
>
> 9. *Gives feedback to learners*
>
> 12. *Handles problem learners*

2. Identify

Underdeveloped or unobserved competencies	Knowledge, skills, and attitudes to acquire
Facilitates exercises	*Sets up activities and conducts a debriefing*
Uses role play	*Sets up role plays and clearly states the objective; summarizes and demonstrates skills*
Administers tests and evaluates skill performance	*Learning the benefits of testing and designing meaningful questions*
Conducts learning online	*Uses online tools and facilitates treaded discussions*

3. Identify competencies that require coaching and feedback:

> *Use of role play. This is a difficult competency for me because I'm uncomfortable in role-play situations.*

4. Identify resources required to develop these competencies:

> *classes and feedback*

Target date for re-evaluation:

three months from now

Sample 2: Competency Model Checklists for Facilitator or Coach

The facilitator who filled out this sample has four years in training and facilitation. She has attended two "train-the-trainer" workshops given by a private vender and a training association. She facilitates a combination of soft skills and technical skills sessions.

A = meets *advanced* competency (advanced tangible results or outputs are visible)

B = meets *basic* competency (tangible results or outputs are visible)

I = *incomplete* (tangible results or outputs are not observed, missing or partially complete)

N = behavior *not* observed (not competent)

Rating	Facilitator Competencies	Basic Results or Output	Advanced Results or Output
A	1. Plans team or training meetings using an agenda	Facilitator's agenda	Collaborative agenda
A	2. Sets a productive climate and begins a discussion	Participants are ready to begin a discussion	Participants are ready to begin a discussion, collaboratively set ground rules
B	3. Gets the group to focus on defining and reaching outcomes	Defined outcomes Plan to reach outcomes	Defined outcomes Plan to reach outcomes Variety of processes to reach outcomes
A	4. Helps group communicate effectively	Effective group communication	Effective group communication Group harmony Open and civil disagreement
A	5. Encourages creative problem solving, including brainstorming	List of brainstormed options Solved problems	List of brainstormed options Variety of problem-solving techniques Solved problems
A	6. Supports and encourage participation	Partial group participation	Complete, non-defensive group participation
A	7. Fosters self-discovery of alternatives and solutions	Participants find alternatives and solutions	Participants find alternatives and solutions Inventories

Rating	Facilitator Competencies	Basic Results or Output	Advanced Results or Output
B	8. Helps the group make decisions	Group makes a decision Facilitator's rationale	Group reaches a decision, by consensus when appropriate Group's rationale
A	9. Selects a team leader	Team leader selected by the facilitator	Team leader selected by the group
B	10. Handles disruptive participants effectively from the group	Problem ignored or problem member excluded	Behavior change

Rating	Coaching Competencies	Basic Results or Output	Advanced Results or Output
A	1. Builds a relationship	Participants accept coaching	Participants willingly accept coaching
A	2. Provides information	Shared expertise	Shared information
B	3. Facilitates development	Participants develop skills	Participants develop skills through self-discovery
B	4. Confronts when necessary	Participants overcome inaction Facilitator removes learning obstacles	Participants overcome inaction Suggests how the learner can remove obstacles
A	5. Deals with change	Change occurs	Change effected successfully

100%	**Total of competencies observed**
75%	**Total required for competence**

(Ten of fifteen competencies [66 percent] are rated "A" and five competencies [33 percent] are rated "B." This facilitator has basic competency and could be considered advanced if two more basic competencies are rated "A.")

Facilitator or Coach Development Plan

Facilitator's or Coach's Name: *Faciltator B* _____ Date: _____

1. List competencies that exceed expectation:

   Plans team or training meetings using an agenda

   Sets a productive climate and begins a discussion

   Helps group communicate effectively

   Encourages creative problem solving, including brainstorming

   Supports and encourages participation

   Fosters self-discovery

2. Identify

Underdeveloped or unobserved competencies	Knowledge, skills, and attitudes to acquire
Gets the group to focus on outcomes	*Greater understanding of group dynamics*
	Better organization of information developed by the group
Helps the group make decisions	*Questioning techniques*
	Help others change their minds
	Better understanding of consensus
Handles disruptive participants effectively	*Better prevention strategies*
	Develop lower-risk strategies
Facilitates development	*Questioning skills*
	Identify better resources
Confronts when necessary	*Encourages learners to identify and remove obstacles for themselves*
	Links rewards to progress and positive behavior

3. Identify competencies that require coaching and feedback:

   Helps groups make decisions

4. Identify resources required to develop these competencies:

   Questioning techniques to make group decisions

Target date for re-evaluation:

four months from now

GLOSSARY

Adult learning climate. The trainer creates a climate that honors an adult's prior knowledge, skills, and attitudes. Learners are treated as colleagues and partners in the learning process.

Advanced competency. Tangible results or outputs are visible at an intermediate or advanced level.

Basic competency. Tangible results or outputs are visible at a basic level.

Centralized training function. All trainers in an organization work in one group with specific trainers acting as internal consultants to specific business units.

Certification program. Demonstration of competency through testing designed around a specific role.

Certificate program. Completion of course work designed around a specific role.

Competency. An observable behavior supported by specific knowledge, skills, and attitudes. Each competency has specific results or output.

Competency measurement. Observing a person in a specific role to identify whether the competency is present at a basic or advanced level with specific results or output visible.

Competency model. A set of competencies for a specific role.

Course designer. This person assesses training needs, develops a training plan, designs training course materials, and tests to meet specific learning objectives that are tied to a business need.

Decentralized training function. Trainers are assigned to a specific business unit and report to an operating manager.

Facilitator. A person who leads a meeting or training program and encourages the group to develop content, answer questions, or solve a problem without over-directing the group.

Instructor. See trainer.

Internal consulting process. A systematic eight-step process used to identify a client's needs and provide appropriate solutions. *See Chapter 6.*

Lesson plan. A trainer's written guide with a description of objectives, activities, job aids, questions, and possible answers to present a training program.

Life cycle of a training department. A cycle that begins with an assessment of a training need related to a business need, followed by a recommended solution and resources. After the solution is implemented, expertise is built and, if success is demonstrated to management, support for the training department will be maintained. If expertise is not built and success is not demonstrated, management support is withdrawn and the function is reduced to a survival mode and ends.

Needs assessment. Gathering of information about a specific business need that can be resolved by training. The many types of needs assessments include performance analysis, target population analysis, sorting training needs and wants, job analysis, and task analysis.

Performance skill checklist. A checklist of skills matched to learning objectives and used to observe a person demonstrate competency.

Skill hierarchy. An arrangement of skills that shows dependence of one skill on another.

Target population. The individuals or group involved in a needs assessment or training program.

Trainer. This person presents information and directs structured learning experiences so individuals increase their knowledge and skills. This person can also act as a performance coach and facilitator.

Training function. A department in an organization that meets training and development needs, conducts needs assessments, designs and delivers training courses to meet business needs. The function can be centralized or decentralized and can be staffed by full-time or part-time staff. In some cases, the function may not be a separate department and may report to an operational department.

Training coordinator. Person responsible for the administrative support of the training function.

Training manager. Person responsible for the overall operation of a training function who has strategic and tactical responsibilities.

Training plan. Based on a needs assessment, a training plan identifies training issues, recommends results and objectives, and suggests how they can be reached. The plan states the causes of a deficiency, what performance standards are not being met, and who is the target population. The plan further recommends a means to evaluate suggested strategies, how to partner with management, and when interventions are to be scheduled.

BIBLIOGRAPHY

ASTD 2004 Competency Study: Mapping the Future. New workplace learning and performance competencies. Alexandria, VA: ASTD.

Barner, Robert. "Five Steps to Leadership Competencies." *Training & Development,* March 2000, pp. 47–51.

Benson, George. "Is Training Different Across the Border?" *Training & Development,* October 1997, pp. 57–58.

Birch, Daniel. "e-Learner Competencies." *ASTD Learning Circuits,* July 2002.

Block, Peter. *Flawless Consulting: A Guide to Getting Your Expertise Used* (2nd ed.). San Francisco: Pfeiffer, 2000.

Brethower, Dale, & Smalley, Karolyn. *Performance-Based Instruction: Linking Training to Business Results.* San Francisco: Pfeiffer, 1998.

CIPD Professional Standards, Certificate in Training Practice, UK. www.cipd.co.uk

Colteryahn, Karen, & Davis, Patty. "Trends You Need to Know Now." *Training & Development,* January 2004, pp. 28–36.

Conway, Mal. "Evaluating Trainer Effectiveness." *ASTD Info-Line,* March 2001.

Dalton, Maxine. "Are Competency Models a Waste?" *Training & Development,* October 1997, pp. 46–49.

Davis, Patty, Naughton, Jennifer, & Rothwell, William. "New Roles and New Competencies for the Profession." *Training & Development,* April 2004, pp. 26–36.

Cook, Marshall J. *Effective Coaching.* New York: McGraw-Hill, 1999.

DDI. "How Do You Stack Up Next to Training's New Guard?" *Training & Development,* May 1997.

Dent, Janice. "Fundamentals of HIP." *ASTD Info-Line,* November 1998.

Dubois, David, & Rothwell, William. "Competency-Based or a Traditional Approach to Training." *Training & Development,* April 2004, pp. 46–56.

Eline, Leanne. "A Trainer's Guide to Skill Building." *Technical Training,* September/October 1998, pp. 34–41.

Filipczak, Bob. "Certifiable!" *Training,* August 1995.

Frankola, Karen. "Training e-Trainers." *ASTD Learning Circuits,* August 2001.

Galagan, Pat. "The Future of the Profession Formerly Known as Training." *Training & Development,* December 2003, pp. 28–38.

Green, P.C. *Building Robust Competencies: Linking Human Resource Systems to Organizational Strategies.* San Francisco: Jossey-Bass, 1999.

Hale, Judith. *Performance-Based Certification.* San Francisco: Pfeiffer, 2000.

Huequet, Marc. "The New Trainer." *Training,* December 1995, pp. 23–29.

International Board of Standards for Training, Performance, and Instruction (IBSTPI). *Instructor Competencies* (1993 and 2003), *Instructional Design Competencies* (1986 and 2000), *Training Manager Competencies* (1989 and 2001).* www.ibstpi.org.

Kaner, Sam, Lind, Lenny, Toldi, Catherine, Fisk, Sarah, & Berger, Duane. *Facilitator's Guide to Participatory Decision Making.* Gabriola Island, BC: New Society Publishers, 1996.

Kenny, John B. *Competency Analysis for Trainers: A Personal Planning Guide.* Toronto: Ontario Society for Training & Development, 1979.

Kirkpatrick, Donald L. *Evaluating Training Programs: The Four Levels* (2nd ed.). San Francisco: Berrett-Koehler, 1998.

Langdon, Danny, & Whiteside, Kathleen. "Bringing Sense to Competency Definition and Attainment." *Performance Improvement,* 43(7),10–15, August 2004.

Lee, Chris. "Certified to Train." *Training,* September 1998, pp. 32–40.

Lucia, Antionette, & Lepsinger, Richard. *The Art and Science of Competency Models.* San Francisco: Pfeiffer, 1999.

McLagan, Patricia A. "Competencies: The Next Generation" *Training & Development,* May 1997, pp. 40–47.

McLagan, Patricia A. *Models for Excellence.* Alexandria, VA: ASTD, 1983.

Mulkey, Jamie, & Naughton, Jennifer. "Dispelling the Myths of Certification." *Training & Development,* January 2005, pp. 20-29.

Newman, Amy. "Knowledge Management." *ASTD Info-Line,* March 1999.

Ottawa University. *Core Competency Development Guide,* 1999, available: www.uottawa.ca/services/hr/perf/comp_dev_guide_e.html.

Parry, Scott. "Just What Is a Competency? (And Why Should You Care?)." *Training,* June 1998, p. 64.

Parry, Scott. "The Quest for Competencies." *Training,* July 1996, pp. 48–56.

Phillips, Jack, & Prescott McCoy, Carol (Eds.). *Managing the Small Training Staff.* Alexandria, VA: ASTD, 1998.

Rothwell, William J. *ASTD Models for Human Performance Improvement: Roles, Competencies, and Outputs.* Alexandria, VA: ASTD, 1996.

Rothwell, William J., & Sensenig, Kevin J. (Eds.). *The Sourcebook for Self-Directed* Learning. Amherst, MA: HRD Press, 1999.

Sanders, Ethan S. "e-Learning Competencies." *ASTD Learning Circuits,* March 2001.

Talbet, Karen E. "Generic Competencies: Definition and Application." *ASTD White Paper,* November 2003. www.astd.org.

Thomas, Beth. "How to Hire Instructors Who Live Training." *Training & Development,* March 1999, pp. 14–15.

Training Staff. "Training Today—The Certified Training Department." *Training,* August 1995.

Weinstein, Margot B. "Training 101: Thirty-Three World-Class Competencies." *Training & Development.* May 2000, pp. 20–23.

Zemke, Ron, & Zemke, Susan. "Putting Competencies to Work." *Training,* January 1999, pp. 70–76.

INDEX

Jean Barbazette is the president of The Training Clinic, a training and consulting firm she founded in 1977. Her company focuses on training trainers throughout the United States for major profit, non-profit, and government organizations. The Training Clinic has three international licensees in the Netherlands, Hungary, and Colombia. Prior books include *Successful New Employee Orientation* (2nd ed.) (Pfeiffer, 2001); *The Trainer's Support Handbook* (McGraw-Hill, 2001); and *Instant Case Studies* (Pfeiffer, 2003). She is a frequent contributor to *ASTD Training & Development Sourcebooks, McGraw-Hill Training & Performance Sourcebooks,* and *Pfeiffer Annuals.*

Jean is in the process of developing hard copy and online assessments for trainers, facillitators, coaches, course designers, training managers, and training coordinators based on the competencies in this book. If you would like to participate in validating the assessment at no charge, please contact the author through her website.

Jean Barbazette, President
The Training Clinic
645 Seabreeze Drive
Seal Beach, CA 90740
jean@thetrainingclinic.com
www.thetrainingclinic.com

System Requirements

PC with Microsoft Windows 98SE or later

Mac with Apple OS version 8.6 or later

Using the CD with Windows

To view the items located on the CD, follow these steps:

1. Insert the CD into your computer's CD-ROM drive.

2. A window appears with the following options:

   Contents: Allows you to view the files included on the CD-ROM.

   Software: Allows you to install useful software from the CD-ROM.

   Links: Displays a hyperlinked page of websites.

   Author: Displays a page with information about the Author(s).

   Contact Us: Displays a page with information on contacting the publisher or author.

   Help: Displays a page with information on using the CD.

   Exit: Closes the interface window.

If you do not have autorun enabled, or if the autorun window does not appear, follow these steps to access the CD:

1. Click Start → Run.

2. In the dialog box that appears, type d:\start.exe, where d is the letter of your CD-ROM drive. This brings up the autorun window described in the preceding set of steps.

3. Choose the desired option from the menu. (See Step 2 in the preceding list for a description of these options.)

In Case of Trouble

If you experience difficulty using the CD-ROM, please follow these steps:

1. Make sure your hardware and systems configurations conform to the systems requirements noted under "System Requirements" above.

2. Review the installation procedure for your type of hardware and operating system.

It is possible to reinstall the software if necessary.

To speak with someone in Product Technical Support, call 800-762-208-2974 or 317-208-572-208>3994 M–F 8:30 a.m. – 5:00 p.m. EST. You can also get support and contact Product Technical Support through our website at www.wiley.com/techsupport.

Before calling or writing, please have the following information available:

- Type of computer and operating system
- Any error messages displayed
- Complete description of the problem.

It is best if you are sitting at your computer when making the call.

Pfeiffer Publications Guide

This guide is designed to familiarize you with the various types of Pfeiffer publications. The formats section describes the various types of products that we publish; the methodologies section describes the many different ways that content might be provided within a product. We also provide a list of the topic areas in which we publish.

FORMATS

In addition to its extensive book-publishing program, Pfeiffer offers content in an array of formats, from fieldbooks for the practitioner to complete, ready-to-use training packages that support group learning.

FIELDBOOK Designed to provide information and guidance to practitioners in the midst of action. Most fieldbooks are companions to another, sometimes earlier, work, from which its ideas are derived; the fieldbook makes practical what was theoretical in the original text. Fieldbooks can certainly be read from cover to cover. More likely, though, you'll find yourself bouncing around following a particular theme, or dipping in as the mood, and the situation, dictate.

HANDBOOK A contributed volume of work on a single topic, comprising an eclectic mix of ideas, case studies, and best practices sourced by practitioners and experts in the field.

An editor or team of editors usually is appointed to seek out contributors and to evaluate content for relevance to the topic. Think of a handbook not as a ready-to-eat meal, but as a cookbook of ingredients that enables you to create the most fitting experience for the occasion.

RESOURCE Materials designed to support group learning. They come in many forms: a complete, ready-to-use exercise (such as a game); a comprehensive resource on one topic (such as conflict management) containing a variety of methods and approaches; or a collection of like-minded activities (such as icebreakers) on multiple subjects and situations.

TRAINING PACKAGE An entire, ready-to-use learning program that focuses on a particular topic or skill. All packages comprise a guide for the facilitator/trainer and a workbook for the participants. Some packages are supported with additional media—such as video—or learning aids, instruments, or other devices to help participants understand concepts or practice and develop skills.

- *Facilitator/trainer's guide* Contains an introduction to the program, advice on how to organize and facilitate the learning event, and step-by-step instructor notes. The guide also contains copies of presentation materials—handouts, presentations, and overhead designs, for example—used in the program.

- *Participant's workbook* Contains exercises and reading materials that support the learning goal and serves as a valuable reference and support guide for participants in the weeks and months that follow the learning event. Typically, each participant will require his or her own workbook.

ELECTRONIC CD-ROMs and web-based products transform static Pfeiffer content into dynamic, interactive experiences. Designed to take advantage of the searchability, automation, and ease-of-use that technology provides, our e-products bring convenience and immediate accessibility to your workspace.

METHODOLOGIES

CASE STUDY A presentation, in narrative form, of an actual event that has occurred inside an organization. Case studies are not prescriptive, nor are they used to prove a point; they are designed to develop critical analysis and decision-making skills. A case study has a specific time frame, specifies a sequence of events, is narrative in structure, and contains a plot structure—an issue (what should be/have been done?). Use case studies when the goal is to enable participants to apply previously learned theories to the circumstances in the case, decide what is pertinent, identify the real issues, decide what should have been done, and develop a plan of action.

ENERGIZER A short activity that develops readiness for the next session or learning event. Energizers are most commonly used after a break or lunch to stimulate or refocus the group. Many involve some form of physical activity, so they are a useful way to counter post-lunch lethargy. Other uses include transitioning from one topic to another, where "mental" distancing is important.

EXPERIENTIAL LEARNING ACTIVITY (ELA) A facilitator-led intervention that moves participants through the learning cycle from experience to application (also known as a Structured Experience). ELAs are carefully thought-out designs in which there is a definite learning purpose and intended outcome. Each step—everything that participants do during the activity—facilitates the accomplishment of the stated goal. Each ELA includes complete instructions for facilitating the intervention and a clear statement of goals, suggested group size and timing, materials required, an explanation of the process, and, where appropriate, possible variations to the activity. (For more detail on Experiential Learning Activities, see the Introduction to the *Reference Guide to Handbooks and Annuals*, 1999 edition, Pfeiffer, San Francisco.)

GAME A group activity that has the purpose of fostering team spirit and togetherness in addition to the achievement of a pre-stated goal. Usually contrived—undertaking a desert expedition, for example—this type of learning method offers an engaging means for participants to demonstrate and practice business and interpersonal skills. Games are effective for team building and personal development mainly because the goal is subordinate to the process—the means through which participants reach decisions, collaborate, communicate, and generate trust and understanding. Games often engage teams in "friendly" competition.

ICEBREAKER A (usually) short activity designed to help participants overcome initial anxiety in a training session and/or to acquaint the participants with one another. An icebreaker can be a fun activity or can be tied to specific topics or training goals. While a useful tool in itself, the icebreaker comes into its own in situations where tension or resistance exists within a group.

INSTRUMENT A device used to assess, appraise, evaluate, describe, classify, and summarize various aspects of human behavior. The term used to describe an instrument depends primarily on its format and purpose. These terms include survey, questionnaire, inventory, diagnostic, survey, and poll. Some uses of instruments include providing instrumental feedback to group members, studying here-and-now processes or functioning within a group, manipulating group composition, and evaluating outcomes of training and other interventions.

Instruments are popular in the training and HR field because, in general, more growth can occur if an individual is provided with a method for focusing specifically on his or her own behavior. Instruments also are used to obtain information that will serve as a basis for change and to assist in workforce planning efforts.

Paper-and-pencil tests still dominate the instrument landscape with a typical package comprising a facilitator's guide, which offers advice on administering the instrument and interpreting the collected data, and an initial set of instruments. Additional instruments are available separately. Pfeiffer, though, is investing heavily in e-instruments. Electronic instrumentation provides effortless distribution and, for larger groups particularly, offers advantages over paper-and-pencil tests in the time it takes to analyze data and provide feedback.

LECTURETTE A short talk that provides an explanation of a principle, model, or process that is pertinent to the participants' current learning needs. A lecturette is intended to establish a common language bond between the trainer and the participants by providing a mutual frame of reference. Use a lecturette as an introduction to a group activity or event, as an interjection during an event, or as a handout.

MODEL A graphic depiction of a system or process and the relationship among its elements. Models provide a frame of reference and something more tangible, and more easily remembered, than a verbal explanation. They also give participants something to "go on," enabling them to track their own progress as they experience the dynamics, processes, and relationships being depicted in the model.

ROLE PLAY A technique in which people assume a role in a situation/scenario: a customer service rep in an angry-customer exchange, for example. The way in which the role is approached is then discussed and feedback is offered. The role play is often repeated using a different approach and/or incorporating changes made based on feedback received. In other words, role playing is a spontaneous interaction involving realistic behavior under artificial (and safe) conditions.

SIMULATION A methodology for understanding the interrelationships among components of a system or process. Simulations differ from games in that they test or use a model that depicts or mirrors some aspect of reality in form, if not necessarily in content. Learning occurs by studying the effects of change on one or more factors of the model. Simulations are commonly used to test hypotheses about what happens in a system—often referred to as "what if?" analysis—or to examine best-case/worst-case scenarios.

THEORY A presentation of an idea from a conjectural perspective. Theories are useful because they encourage us to examine behavior and phenomena through a different lens.

TOPICS

The twin goals of providing effective and practical solutions for workforce training and organization development and meeting the educational needs of training and human resource professionals shape Pfeiffer's publishing program. Core topics include the following:

Leadership & Management

Communication & Presentation

Coaching & Mentoring

Training & Development

E-Learning

Teams & Collaboration

OD & Strategic Planning

Human Resources

Consulting

What will you find on pfeiffer.com?

- The best in workplace performance solutions for training and HR professionals

- Downloadable training tools, exercises, and content

- Web-exclusive offers

- Training tips, articles, and news

- Seamless on-line ordering

- Author guidelines, information on becoming a Pfeiffer Affiliate, and much more

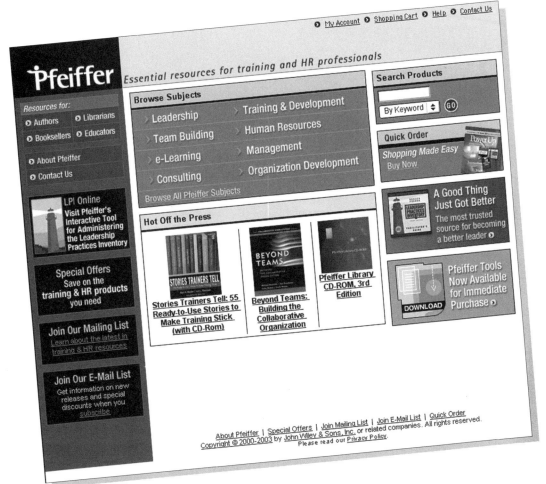

Discover more at www.pfeiffer.com

Customer Care

Have a question, comment, or suggestion? Contact us! We value your feedback and we want to hear from you.

For questions about this or other Pfeiffer products, you may contact us by:

E-mail: **customer@wiley.com**

Mail: **Customer Care Wiley/Pfeiffer**
        10475 Crosspoint Blvd.
        Indianapolis, IN 46256

Phone: **(US) 800-274-4434** (Outside the US: 317-572-3985)

Fax: **(US) 800-569-0443** (Outside the US: 317-572-4002)

To order additional copies of this title or to browse other Pfeiffer products, visit us online at **www.pfeiffer.com**.

For **Technical Support** questions call **(800) 274-4434.**

For authors guidelines, log on to www.pfeiffer.com and click on "Resources for Authors."

If you are . . .

A **college bookstore, a professor, an instructor, or work in higher education** and you'd like to place an order or request an exam copy, please contact jbreview@wiley.com.

A **general retail bookseller** and you'd like to establish an account or speak to a local sales representative, contact Melissa Grecco at 201-748-6267 or mgrecco@wiley.com.

An **exclusively on-line bookseller**, contact Amy Blanchard at 530-756-9456 or ablanchard @wiley.com or Jennifer Johnson at 206-568-3883 or jjohnson@wiley.com, both of our Online Sales department.

A **librarian or library representative**, contact John Chambers in our Library Sales department at 201-748-6291 or jchamber@wiley.com.

A **reseller, training company/consultant, or corporate trainer**, contact Charles Regan in our Special Sales department at 201-748-6553 or cregan@wiley.com.

A **specialty retail distributor** (includes specialty gift stores, museum shops, and corporate bulk sales), contact Kim Hendrickson in our Special Sales department at 201-748-6037 or khendric@wiley.com.

Purchasing for the **Federal government**, contact Ron Cunningham in our Special Sales department at 317-572-3053 or rcunning@wiley.com.

Purchasing for a **State or Local government**, contact Charles Regan in our Special Sales department at 201-748-6553 or cregan@wiley.com.